Strategic Planning

Strategic Planning

Fundamentals for Small Business

Gary L. May

Strategic Planning: Fundamentals for Small Business
Copyright © Business Expert Press, LLC, 2010.

First published in 2010 by
Business Expert Press, LLC
222 East 46th Street, New York, NY 10017
www.businessexpertpress.com

ISBN-13: 978-1-60649-086-0 (paperback)
ISBN-10: 1-60649-086-0 (paperback)

ISBN-13: 978-1-60649-087-7 (e-book)
ISBN-10: 1-60649-087-7 (e-book)

DOI 10.4128/9781606490866

A publication in the Business Expert Press Small Business Management and Entrepreneurship collection

Collection ISSN: 1946-5653 (print)
Collection ISSN: 1946-5661 (electronic)

Cover design by Jonathan Pennell
Interior design by Scribe, Inc.

First edition: March 2010

10 9 8 7 6 5 4 3 2 1

Printed in Taiwan R.O.C.

Abstract

This book explains how small-business owners and managers can use strategic planning to gain a competitive edge, earn higher profits, and increase personal satisfaction. Here is the mantra for the small business-person that is the theme of this book: *be focused, be different, and be better.* This book provides simple models and practical illustrations to guide the small-business planning team through the basics of the strategic-planning process. With strategic planning, you can control your destiny and guide your business toward profitable achievement of your vision.

Keywords

Vision, mission, values, external and internal analysis, strategy, tactics

Contents

Introduction

Strategic planning. As a former small business owner, I know what you are thinking: "Strategic planning is for big companies." "It's too academic." "I don't have time." I'll respond by getting straight to the point: Strategy is simply your game plan for gaining a competitive advantage and earning higher profits. Just like a football coach, you need a game plan to win. Strategic planning will help you win in the game of business. The small business team that follows a systematic strategic planning model will experience many other benefits. For example, you will

- be more focused on creating value for your customer, making better use of your time and limited resources,
- experience less crisis management as everyone on your team works together from the same playbook,
- communicate more effectively with your stakeholders, including your customers, investors, and employees,
- increase your ability to manage sustained, profitable growth.

This book is about the fundamentals of strategic planning for the small business owner and his or her leadership team. The U.S. Small Business Administration defines a small business as typically having fewer than 500 employees (for most manufacturing industries) or less than $7 million in average annual sales (for most retail trade and service businesses).[1]

Strategic planning is an essential process for businesses of every size. While large businesses may have more resources and time to devote to strategic planning, small businesses have the ability to move quickly and the advantage of being close to their stakeholders. As a small business leader, you have your hands full juggling many different responsibilities and challenges on a daily basis. Therefore, this book focuses on the basics—the essential concepts and processes your team can follow to efficiently create and execute an effective strategic plan without getting bogged down in excessive formalization and bureaucracy. The discussions

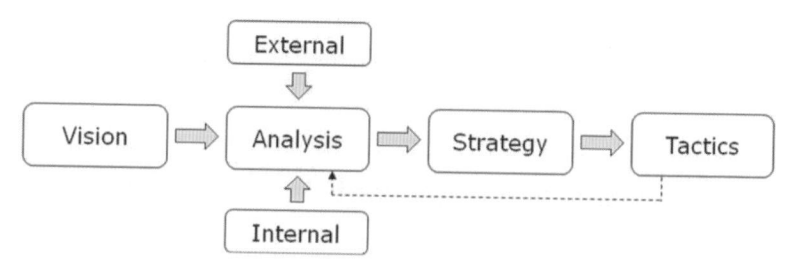

Figure I.1. *The strategic-planning process.*

provide examples from different types of small businesses drawn from my small business experience, consulting clients, and the business press. I also use a case study through the book, featuring a specialty food distributor, to help integrate the various principles and concepts. The model shown (Figure I.1) outlines the template for this book.

The first chapter explains how to articulate a clear vision and mission and how to create a set of values for your business that point to the future and provide a decision-making framework. The second and third chapters provide the analysis questions you need to think about as you scan your environment to identify external and internal factors that may influence your strategic decisions. The fourth chapter outlines the most common business strategies and the rationale for each. The final chapter addresses tactical planning, the practical aspects of ensuring good execution of your strategic initiatives, measuring success, and communicating your strategy.

While the model appears linear in nature, the fast pace of change in our global economy requires an ongoing review process, with a periodic evaluation of assumptions against the realties of the marketplace, hence the loop from tactics back to analysis. No strategy can be cast in stone. While vision, mission, and core values remain constant over long periods, business strategies and tactics must adapt to an evolving world.

Following this model will help move your organization toward profitable achievement of your business vision. Research supports this conclusion. Small business owner-managers who use strategic management tools outperform those who manage by the seat of their pants.[2] Use this book to help achieve the desired future for your business.

CHAPTER 1

Vision, Mission, and Values

Every business needs a vision, a mission, and clear values. Vision provides the long-term perspective and your reason for being—*why* you are in business. Mission clarifies your operating focus—*what* you do. Values provide a framework for behavior—*how* you do it. You cannot delegate the development of these three elements. They are the responsibility of the owner and his or her senior leadership team. Defining vision, mission, and values represents the essence of leadership, which is setting direction and motivating others to pursue that direction.

Articulating Your Vision

The first step in a journey is to determine your destination. As Yogi Berra said, "If you don't know where you are going, you might wind up someplace else."[1] Where do you want your business to be 5 years, 10 years, even 15 years from now? What do you want to be known for? Why does your business exist? The answers to these questions can provide inspiration to your associates and open everyone's eyes to possibilities. We all have a need to be a part of something significant and meaningful.

You started, acquired, or agreed to lead a small business because you have a desire to control your own destiny and to make a difference serving a need in the marketplace. At the root of the decision was a passion for achieving a picture of the future that was in your mind. However, you could not manifest that passion alone. You recruited others who shared at the gut level your vision, and you began building the business together. There was not time for hanging vision statements on the wall.

Why should you take the time now to codify your vision? First, as your business grows, you need to communicate the vision to new members of your organization in a systematic manner. Second, a clear business vision improves organizational performance and helps attract talented people. Mark Lipton, in his article "Demystifying the Development of an Organizational Vision," references more than 30 studies that validate the positive organizational and financial impact of a well-crafted vision.[2] According to Lipton, a vision benefits a company in five ways:

1. Provides the basis for a strategic plan
2. Motivates individuals and facilitates the recruitment of talent
3. Helps keep decision making in context
4. Facilitates needed change
5. Enhances a wide range of performance measures

What does a meaningful vision look and sound like? If you look at the literature on vision, you will find examples of vision statements that run several paragraphs long. Often you will find vision models that incorporate multiple elements. My recommendation for the small business owner is simplicity. Some of the most brilliant and charismatic founders of businesses expressed their vision for the future in one simple sentence. Here are some examples from the field of technology:[3]

- "Organize the world's information and make it universally accessible and useful" (Larry Page and Sergey Brin, Google)
- "A personal computer in every home running Microsoft software" (Bill Gates, Microsoft)
- "To be the earth's most customer-centric company; to build a place where people can come to find and discover anything they might want to buy online" (Jeff Bezos, Amazon)

While these businesses are now, of course, huge corporations and market leaders, remember that they started small—with a vision. Interestingly, Jeff Bezos has a new vision to support his venture for electronic books and the Kindle electronic book reader: "Our vision is every book ever printed in any language all available in 60 seconds."[4] Wow! It may take years to achieve, but can you see how such a vision will inspire employees and drive the business forward?

For a more down-to-earth example, we can look to renowned restaurateur Alice Waters, who founded the Chez Panisse restaurant in Berkeley, California, in 1971. Waters's vision of helping others "learn the vital relationship of food to agriculture and of food to culture, and how food affects the quality of our everyday lives" not only fueled her commercial success, but also launched a sociopolitical movement.[5] Her support of organic practices, her close relationships with area farmers and other suppliers, and her unwavering commitment to quality made her business a model for the power of fresh, simply prepared food and contributed to the business world's new focus on sustainability and environmental awareness.

Table 1.1 provides example vision statements from other small businesses. All share the common characteristics of an effective vision, stating what a business hopes to become and stretching the imagination in a simple, inspirational manner.

The responsibility for articulating the vision belongs to you and your leadership team. This activity is not a large group exercise. You must sit down with your team, with flip chart paper or whiteboard, and talk it out. In their article "Building Your Company's Vision," Jim Collins and Jerry Porras suggest one method for teasing out the root of your business vision:

One powerful method for getting at purpose is the *five whys*. Start with a descriptive statement We make X products or We deliver X services, and then ask, Why is that important? five times. After a few whys, you'll find that you're getting down to the fundamental purpose of the organization.[6]

Table 1.1. Example Vision Statements From Small Businesses

Type of business	Vision statement
Construction	To build with such excellence that we become the premier commercial contractor in the Big City metro area, known for our contribution to the quality of life at work through our innovative building designs and environmentally friendly building practices.
School of business	To become recognized throughout the southeast for the high quality of our programs, the quality of our graduates, and our willingness to meet the needs of our business community.
Produce distributor	To help families in Main Town live happier and healthier lives by providing the freshest, tastiest, and most nutritious local produce.
Nonprofit ministry	To teach young girls of color how to discover their dream.

For example, the senior team of our case study, a privately held specialty food distributor we will call Serv-Pro (not its real name), began by saying, "We distribute and service specialty and gourmet food products in supermarkets."[7] After a series of whys, they concluded that their services are important to the retailer because "we give shoppers the variety they desire at the lowest total system cost and the highest return on investment for the retailer." The vision statement that ultimately emerged from this introspection was simple but powerful: "Our vision is to surprise and delight the supermarket shopper with the best variety of creatively merchandised specialty food products, creating happy retailers and satisfied stakeholders."

Other questions that can be adapted to stimulate your group's visionary thinking include the following:[8]

- Why did we start (or buy) this business?
- What would be lost if the company ceased to exist?
- How could we frame the purpose of this organization so that if you won the lottery tomorrow with enough money to retire, you would nevertheless keep working here?
- What deeper sense of purpose would motivate you to continue to dedicate your creative energies to this company's efforts?
- If someone writes an article for a major business magazine about this company 15 years from now, what will it say?
- For whose benefit are all our efforts?
- What major contribution will we make to the lives of our stakeholders?
- Where do we want to be in 5 to 10 years?

Notice that in all this discussion about vision and purpose, there is little mention of profit. Peter Drucker, one of the greatest management thinkers, reminds us that, while profit is necessary, it is not the purpose, but rather a test of the validity of an organization's reason for existence and its business strategy.[9] Committing your working life to a business just so it can make profit or increase shareholder value does not inspire.

Clarifying Your Mission

A vision draws a picture of a desired future and articulates the ultimate purpose of your business—why it exists. Mission flows from vision and is more concrete. Mission answers questions about what the business does.[10] For example, here are the original vision and mission statements of the nonprofit organization Big Brothers Big Sisters of America:[11]

Vision: To make a positive difference in the lives of children and youth so that they will achieve their highest potential.

Mission: Providing and supporting committed volunteers who have one-to-one relationships with children and youth.

Do you see how their vision explains *why* the organization exists and how the mission statement clarifies *what* the Big Brothers Big Sisters organization actually does in pursuit of their vision?

Peter Drucker reminds us that the customer should define the business.[12] To satisfy the customer is the ultimate mission of every business. An effective mission statement is customer oriented and market focused. To help clarify the mission, it helps to answer four questions: Who is the customer? Where is the customer? What does the customer buy? How do we satisfy the customer's needs?[13] Figure 1.1 illustrates these four dimensions of the mission statement.

"Who is the customer we want to satisfy?" is the first and most crucial question. Sometimes it is not an easy question to answer. Often we have multiple customers. Returning to our specialty food distributor example, the ultimate customer for the specialty and gourmet foods Serv-Pro distributes is the shopper in the store—the consumer. But the retailer is also a customer. Without the retailer's support and shelf space, the distributor has no business. But what type of retailers? Supermarkets? Convenience stores? Health food stores? Discount department stores? Each type of retail outlet has different needs and expectations. Serv-Pro's decisions on customer focus will, in large measure, define the business.

The question of "Where is the customer?" has to do with the location of your customer, which, in turn, determines the geographic coverage of your business. If the specialty distributor chooses to serve regional

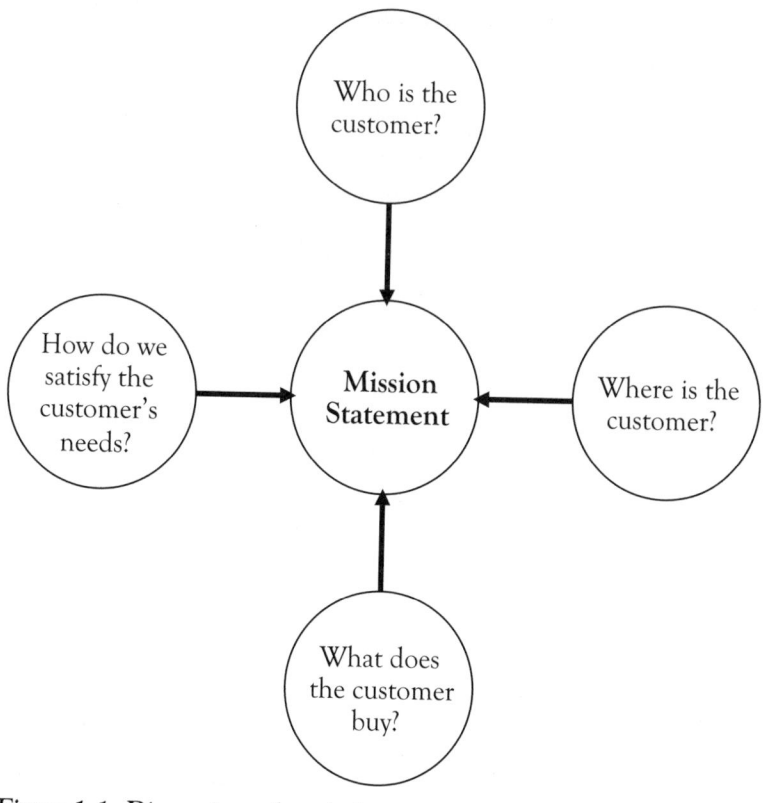

Figure 1.1. Dimensions of a mission statement.

supermarket chains, for example, then the company will have to build a distribution system to support a multistate operation.

The next question, "What does the customer buy?" has to do with the needs that your product or service satisfies. Here is an important truth when defining your business: the customer never buys a product or a service. The customer buys the satisfaction of a want or need. The customer buys *value*—benefits in context of price. This truth is a crucial distinction. Business history is littered with the wreckage of businesses that did not define themselves in terms of what their customers were really buying. The classic examples are the railroads, who thought they were in the railroad business instead of the transportation business, and the manufacturers of typewriters, such as Smith Corona and Underwood, who thought they were selling typewriters instead of satisfying customers' information processing needs. Note also that the value equation for most customers is not just about price. An electrical contractor, for example, may choose to purchase a circuit breaker box that is higher in price because it is engineered to be installed easily by relatively unskilled labor. Reducing the total cost of the product, which includes the cost of labor for installation, is what represents value for the contractor. Another example, cited by Drucker, is the highway construction firm that buys lubricating compounds for heavy earthmoving equipment. For the construction firm, value is "keeping very expensive equipment operating without breakdowns."[14] The choice of lubricant supplier is based more on the quality of lubricants and the speed and dependability of the supplier's onsite service than on price.

From the perspective of our case study, Serv-Pro, the shopper has a number of needs he or she may be satisfying when buying specialty foods: the desire to eat more healthy foods or to entertain guests with something different, or even the convenience of purchasing all the weekly food needs with one-stop shopping. The retailer, of course, is interested in satisfying his customers but wants to make a profit too. However, most retailers today are sophisticated enough to know that the purchase price of a product is only the beginning of the profit equation. A supermarket chain certainly can buy the product, often at a lower price, directly from the manufacturer or through other distributor sources. But the ultimate goal for the retailer is a satisfactory *return on investment*, which factors in all acquisition, handling, and ownership costs along with the productivity of space and capital.

The final question is about how the customers' needs will be satisfied. To generate the desired return on investment for the retailer, Serv-Pro, as a specialized distributor, is not selling product or price. The company is selling logistic and supply chain services and retail merchandising services that generate higher product sales (indicating shopper satisfaction). Serv-Pro achieves the sales with lower total system costs, in less space, and with lower inventories than typical direct-buy options. That is how this distributor satisfies the retailer's desire for a better return on investment.

Given this discussion, here is the resulting mission statement for Serv-Pro:

Our mission is to satisfy the specialty and gourmet food needs of the supermarket shopper while improving the return on invested capital and space for our retail supermarket customers in the New England states. We meet the needs of our shoppers and our retailers through innovative logistical and supply-chain solutions and customized retail merchandising services.

It is not essential to be formulistic here, but most effective mission statements incorporate the elements in Figure 1.1 in one form or another. Table 1.2 lists other examples of small business mission statements. Remember that needs can usually be served in many different ways, and a broad customer-oriented business definition safeguards a business from the trap of "selling typewriters" while the market is evolving to systems that provide "information processing."

One other point before we move to a discussion of values—the importance of focus. We will discuss this issue more in the chapter on strategy, but I want to stress the importance of focus for the small business in terms of the mission statement. There is never enough time, people, or

Table 1.2. Example Mission Statements From Small Businesses

Type of business	Mission statement
Construction	We build Class A commercial office buildings for high-end tenants in the Big City metro area, delivering projects to specifications, on time, and on budget using our proprietary total quality management system.
School of business	• *Prepare* a diverse student body for business and professional careers by providing a quality education. • *Provide* a student-centered environment, using technology to enhance student learning. • *Support* faculty in applied and instructional research and service to the profession. • *Serve* primarily the southern metropolitan Atlanta area.
Produce distributor	We link the local farmer with Main Town grocers and restaurants, providing the freshest produce in a timely manner through our state-of-the-art distribution system.
Nonprofit ministry	We design and deliver educational materials that help young girls of color everywhere begin their journey toward fulfillment of their dreams.

money to be everything to everybody. An essential element of strategy is making hard choices. Strategy is as much about what you say no to as what you decide to pursue. My experience has been that small businesses that have a relatively narrow mission focus but deliver with excellence prosper the most (and have the fewest headaches). Over time, as the companies grow, they may revisit and expand their mission, but their initial success is always due to their laser-like focus. One case in point is Jennifer Kahnweiler's leadership consulting business called AboutYOU, based in Atlanta, Georgia. Kahnweiler's company mission is to "build strong leaders through a variety of customized and highly engaging presentations, including keynotes, seminars, workshops, and coaching." Her particular customer focus is on "developing the 50% of aspiring and emerging leaders who are introverted in temperament"—a brilliantly selected market niche. According to Kahnweiler, "We help these high potential contributors to manage their introversion and learn to succeed in an extroverted business world."[15]

Tate Chalk provides another example of the power of focus. Chalk is the founder and owner of Nfinity, a company that makes athletic shoes specifically for women. In an industry dominated by Nike, Reebok, and Adidas, Nfinity has carved out a small but profitable niche with $5 million annual sales, focusing initially on the competitive cheerleading market. Now Chalk is designing shoes for women's basketball and volleyball players. The company has grown methodically, with limited overhead, modest offices, and only eight employees. "We've been very careful to stay focused," Chalk says, "concentrating on an unmet need: producing performance athletic shoes engineered for women competing in team sports. We addressed the physiological and weight differences. For the big guys, these are basically fringe markets."[16]

Establishing Core Values

Core values represent the shared beliefs among the employees of an organization. Values drive an organization's culture, priorities, and behavior. They provide guiding principles that help individuals make decisions, solve problems, and take actions that are consistent with the vision and mission of the business.

Organizational values can be an important source of competitive advantage. For example, Chick-fil-A, Inc., a quick-serve food chain known for its chicken sandwich, is one of the most productive and profitable operators in the restaurant industry. Chick-fil-A's competitive advantage is based in part on the quality and productivity of its store employees who provide "second mile" service, an anomaly in the fast food industry. Truett Cathy, the company's founder, maintains that Chick-fil-A's success is a direct result of its core values, such as "people first," which shape how it treats its employees and customers.[17]

As with Truett Cathy's example, core values for businesses usually reflect the deeply held beliefs of the organization's founders and are independent of the current business environment and management fads. As central beliefs, they are few in number (usually three to five) and can stand the test of time. One way to determine whether a value is core is to ask, "If circumstances changed and penalized us for holding this core value, would we still keep it?" If you cannot honestly answer yes, then the value is not core.[18] Table 1.3 provides a few examples of values that some companies have chosen to be in their core.[19] Remember that values are unique to each company. There is no universally right set of core values. Remember also to

Table 1.3. Example Core Value Statements From Small Businesses

Value	Value statement
Accountability	We take responsibility for our attitudes, actions, and results.
Collaboration	We work together in a spirit of teamwork to serve others.
Communications	We promote honest and continuous two-way communication.
Continuous improvement	We continuously improve all aspects of our business.
Customer focus	We listen to the customer.
Ethical conduct	We always act with integrity.
Innovation	We encourage and support creativity and continuous learning.
People	We treat people for what they are—our most valuable asset.
Quality	We will focus on getting better before trying to get bigger.
Social responsibility	We will support civic activities to improve the quality of life in our communities.

keep them few and simple. A winning culture is defined by words so simple and basic it is easy for everyone to grasp their meaning and importance.

As with the vision and mission statements, the leadership team must spend time together talking through their belief systems to identify their unique set of core values. Collins and Porras suggest thinking through the following questions:[20]

- What core values do you personally bring to your work (these should be so fundamental that you would hold them regardless of whether or not they were rewarded)?
- What would you tell your children are the core values that you hold at work and that you hope they will hold when they become working adults?
- If you awoke tomorrow morning with enough money to retire for the rest of your life, would you continue to live those core values?
- Would you want to hold those core values, even if at some point, one or more of them became a competitive disadvantage?
- If you were to start a new organization tomorrow in a different line of work, what core values would you build into the new organization, regardless of its industry?

Walking the Talk

After you have articulated your vision, clarified your mission, and established your core values, you will most likely put some framed documents on the wall, create some laminated cards for the employees, and maybe even deliver a PowerPoint presentation at a company meeting explaining the significance of the words. While such actions are all well and good, the most important thing for you to do is to set about making sure the core values are a reality in the day-to-day life of your organization. The research on building a winning business culture is clear in this regard: *It is not what you say, it is what you do*. You have to "walk the talk" as you communicate the message over and over again.

First, of course, you will use the vision/mission/values components to guide the development of your strategic plan—a topic in subsequent chapters. In addition, there are five primary ways leaders reinforce their desired culture and the behavior of the organization: attending, reacting, modeling, rewarding, and selecting.[21]

Attending means you spend time and attention on what your values say are important. Our calendar always reveals our priorities. For example, if you talk about the importance of employee development and continuous learning, then your employees should see you attending and even participating in company training activities. *Reacting* has to do with how you respond to problems and crises. If you advocate the value of innovation and creativity, and an employee tries something outside the box that creates a mess, how will you react? If you publicly berate and humiliate the employee, you can be sure other employees will get the message that playing it safe is what is really valued. *Modeling* means that you consistently demonstrate the company values in your own behavior. If collaborating with others in decision making is a company value, and you unilaterally make decisions without consulting those who will be impacted, what message does that send? Who is *rewarded* in the organization, both in terms of promotions and recognition, also sends a powerful message as to what behaviors are really important. Finally, recruiting and *selecting* people for your organization who embody your company values communicates the company's commitment to strengthen the values. The senior leadership must be exemplars in all things related to vision, mission, and values.

In closing this chapter, I would like to share a personal story that illustrates the power of walking the talk. After World War II, my father founded a wholesale business in the basement of our home with a $240 investment. The business distributed and serviced health and beauty care and general merchandise items to small independent grocers in the Atlanta area. I grew up working in the business, and by the time I joined the company full time after college, the business had grown significantly, serving customers throughout the state of Georgia. Dad was a classic entrepreneur, a hard-driving "square peg through the round hole" type of guy who lived the core values of keeping one's word, listening to the customer, and operating with absolute integrity (a rarity in the wholesale business in those days). After spending a number of years working in each of the business functions, I assumed responsibility for sales, human resources, and data processing. The business continued to grow into a multistate operation, and by that time, we were servicing some large regional supermarket chains.

One day our data processing manager informed me that we had a problem. During the process of upgrading to a new computer system, there had been a programming error, and unknowingly, we had been adding a penny to every line item extension on every invoice for about a month. Now, we carried 35,000 items and a retailer's typical invoice would run many pages—that represented a lot of pennies. I decided we needed to bring my dad in on the discussion. The data processing manager explained again what happened, noted that the error had been corrected, and recommended we do nothing else since the error was hidden and had not been noticed by anyone. Dad slammed his hand on the desk and said, "Absolutely not." He instructed the data processing manager to write a program to identify how much we had overcharged each customer and to generate a check to each customer. He instructed me to write a letter of apology to each customer and to prepare our sales management team to hand deliver the checks and letters to every single customer, and he and I would personally take the checks to our largest customers. I thought I was going to die! The typical net profit margin in the supermarket business is a penny on a dollar, and most operators will kill for that penny, especially where wholesalers are concerned. Most checks were small, but for the larger chains, some of the checks were significant. Our sales people thought we were crazy and predicted Armageddon. But within a few short days, we all were on the road delivering checks, hand signed by my dad.

The reaction from the customers, even the regional chains, was incredible. They were amazed. Rather than being angry, they expressed appreciation and profound respect that a distributor would do such a thing. Word spread quickly throughout our territory. Many of our employees expressed their own gratitude for the opportunity to work with a company with such integrity. It was electric. Needless to say, our competitors had a tough time taking our customers from that point on, and our business growth accelerated as retailers were eager to sign on with a distributor they could trust.

The point of the story is clear. From then on, there was never a question in our company about what integrity and honesty meant. My dad modeled the way. It is not what you say, it is what you do.

CHAPTER 2

External Analysis

Your vision and mission provide direction—where you want to go with your business. The next step in the formulation of your strategy—how you are going to get there—is to spend some time thinking about the external business environment and your internal capabilities. This chapter will help you consider the external factors and the potential threats and opportunities that may influence your plan. Chapter 3 will show you how to analyze your internal strengths and weaknesses, factors that will need your attention as you develop strategic initiatives and tactics.

Examining the external environment is important because trends in society, such as changes in demographics or technology, can significantly influence the performance of your company. Forces within your industry, such as the entry of a new competitor, can have a direct impact on your profitability. While you cannot control these external events, you can use the information in the development of your strategy, seeking to minimize threats and take advantage of potential opportunities.

The process of external analysis provides a good opportunity to involve the various stakeholders in your business in the strategic planning process.[1] Every business has groups that have a stake in the success of your business, including customers, employees, suppliers, investors, and community leaders. You need their input and the variety of perspectives they can provide. In addition, you need their commitment for your business to be successful. Inclusion and participation can help build commitment. As Mary Kay Ash, the founder of Mary Kay Cosmetics, said, "People support what they help create."[2]

One approach to involving stakeholders is to create small, informal groups of advisors for your strategic planning effort, people representative of their respective stakeholder groups that you trust and feel comfortable with bouncing around ideas. You want to include individuals who are thought leaders and whose input and support are essential for your success. You also want diversity in the membership of your advisory group, a variety of personalities, backgrounds, and philosophies. For example, Serv-Pro, our privately held specialty food distributor introduced in chapter 1, created the following panels of advisors:

- Customers (consisting of both retailers and shoppers)
- Employees and managers (cross-functional representation)
- Suppliers
- Political and community leaders
- Professors from the business school of a local university

The CEO assigned a senior leader to meet with each of the groups several times to gather their insights on external trends. In the same manner, you can assign each member of your senior team to meet with one of your stakeholder advisory groups to explore the type of questions discussed in this chapter and bring back the information to share with the strategic planning team. Do not make this process complicated. A few informal breakfast meetings, a good set of thought questions provided in advance, and a flip chart for taking notes is all that is required.

In addition to the use of advisors, you and your senior leadership team should be reading business periodicals, such as the *Wall Street Journal*, *Fortune*, and *BusinessWeek*, along with periodicals related to your industry. Membership in trade associations and participation in industry-specific meetings and conferences are other ways to stay in touch with the trends in your larger environment. Many trade associations conduct research and publish periodic reports detailing the state of the industry and future trends. Local business schools are also a good source of information.

Figure 2.1 provides a useful way to think about the environmental factors that surround your business, dividing the analysis into three dimensions: the general or macro environment, your industry, and your direct competitors.

We will look briefly at each of these dimensions and identify some questions you need to think about and talk about with your strategic advisor teams. While these dimensions may be outside your direct control, changes can affect your business. Not all the elements within a dimension

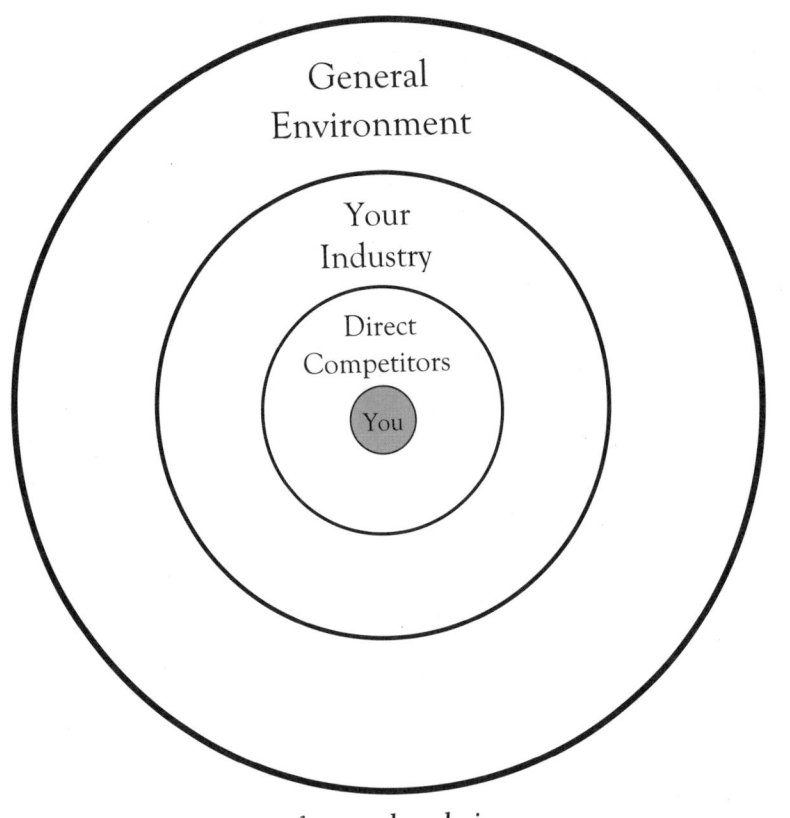

Figure 2.1. Dimensions of external analysis.

may apply to your business, but it is a good exercise to think through each. Remember that your purpose is to look for opportunities that you might be able to leverage for competitive advantage and to identify potential threats so you can plan ways to navigate around them. We will use Serv-Pro to provide a common thread of examples through the discussion.

The General Environment

The general environment is composed of trends in broader society. Businesses must pay attention to six types of factors in the general environment: demographic, sociocultural, technological, political/legal, economic, and global. Anticipated changes in any of these forces can affect your strategic choices.[3]

Demographic Factors

Demographic trends reflect changes in the characteristics of a population, such as age, gender, geographic distribution, ethnic mix, and income distribution. A relevant example for almost any business is the aging of the "baby boom" generation, those born from 1946 to the early 1960s. Often referred to as the "pig in the python," as the baby boomers grew up they created a host of opportunities and threats for various businesses. For example, during the 1970s, many boomers were getting married and created an upsurge in demand for home appliances as they moved into their first homes. During the 1990s, they started to save for retirement, generating massive inflows of money into the mutual fund industry. Now boomers are retiring, creating a demand for more retirement communities and providing opportunities for businesses that cater to older people, such as home health care.

Another example of a powerful demographic trend is the increasing Hispanic population in the United States. As the youngest and fastest-growing ethnic group in the United States, Hispanic purchasing power will influence many firms' decisions about the types of products and services they will sell to serve those needs. For example, our specialty food distributor's early expansion into Hispanic food displays in supermarkets located in areas with increasing Hispanic population paid dividends in sales growth and customer satisfaction. A business school in Serv-Pro's operating area provides another example. Faculty research provided statistics showing a steadily increasing trend of Hispanic students enrolling in public universities in the school's marketing area, with Hispanic enrollment expected to account for over 24% of the college student population by 2022. This trend has obvious implications for the school in terms of developing programs and services to attract and keep that demographic segment of students.

Here is a demographic question for your advisory groups: *What are the demographic trends in our marketing area, and how will these trends influence how we sell and what we sell in the future?*

Sociocultural Factors

Sociocultural trends reflect changes in a society's attitudes, behaviors, and cultural values. For example, one significant movement in recent years has been the trend toward greater health consciousness in many countries around the world. Tapping into the early stages of this trend, our specialty food distributor gained market share and new account penetration by being the first to prominently display and promote healthy foods and beverages in its supermarket accounts.

Another example of a sociocultural trend is the green or environmental movement, which *New York Times* writer Thomas Friedman has called "the next great global industry."[4] Consumers will favor products and services that contribute to a clean environment and energy independence. Businesses that can deliver creative and efficient solutions will have many growth opportunities. Glenn Farris, the founder of Biomass Gas & Electric, is one example of an entrepreneur in the forefront of the "green" energy movement. He pioneered production of electricity for utility companies, municipalities, and businesses through carbon-neutral processes, using a variety of organic fuels such as wood waste to create green power.[5]

Here are the sociocultural questions to share with your advisors: *Do you see any sociocultural trends on the horizon that you believe are important for our business to understand? How should we prepare to deal successfully with these trends?*

Technological Factors

Technological change can be both negative and positive, making a business obsolete overnight and at the same time creating a host of new business opportunities. In particular, Internet-based applications have changed the competitive structures of whole industries. The newspaper industry is one example, experiencing double-digit revenue declines as advertisers have migrated to Web-based media.[6] Imagine what Jeff Bezos's Kindle may do to the book-selling industry. Netflix conceived the business of renting DVDs by mail in the late 1990s as the home video business was shifting to DVDs from VHS tapes, submarining Blockbuster. Now Netflix is scrambling to shift its business to online delivery as DVDs steadily lose ground to movies sent straight over the Internet.[7]

On the other hand, the innovative application of technology to lower costs and improve services can provide significant competitive advantage. Serv-Pro, for example, has invested heavily in bar-code technology such as handheld scanners to lower labor costs, simplify processes, and reduce inventory error costs at the warehouse level. On the retail side, the company uses state-of-the-art digital imaging systems to produce real-time updates to merchandising planograms[8] for their retail service personnel, staying a step ahead of their competitors.

Here are the technology questions for your advisory groups: *What are the technology trends in our industry and related industries that might affect our business? How can we leverage technology to enhance our products, processes, and services?*

Political/Legal Factors

Political and legal forces reflect changes in laws and regulations. Again, these changes can involve both threats and opportunities. The airline deregulation that occurred in 1979 is a classic example, allowing many new airlines to enter the industry. This influx of new competitors led to excess capacity on many routes and resulted in fare wars, damaging the legacy carriers with their expensive hub-and-spoke systems. On a more recent note, many businesses in the United States are wrestling with a cascade of new laws, regulations, and subsidies designed to reduce our dependence on fossil fuels. Health-related regulations provide another example. One local operator of a sports restaurant and bar lost significant business when his county passed an ordinance banning smoking in locations serving food or alcohol.

One regulatory issue that concerns Serv-Pro has to do with vitamins, a product category that historically receives large space allocations in their customers' stores. Not regulated by the Food and Drug Administration (FDA), many of the products make unsupported health claims. The distributor believes that many of these products eventually will become regulated by the FDA, resulting in a dramatic decrease in sales as products are removed from the market. Perceiving the regulation of vitamins as a potential threat, the company is slowly reducing item count and space allocation in selected vitamin categories and keeping inventories low while at the same time looking for new specialty categories they can develop to replace the potential loss of volume.

Here are the political/legal questions for your planning groups: *What are the political and legal trends (national, state, and local) that might affect our business? How can we best track the development of these trends through our legislative and regulatory contacts or through our trade association?*

Economic Factors

Economic factors such as the growth rate of the economy, interest rates, currency exchange rates, and price inflation influence strategic decisions, including whether to increase or shrink capacity. The most obvious example is the negative impact of higher interest rates on the housing market and the sale of big-ticket items such as cars, appliances, and capital equipment. Nevertheless, remember that in any economy, boom or bust, opportunities exist. For example, during the U.S. economic recession that began in 2008, auto-parts distributors and auto repair shops did quite well as consumers repaired their old vehicles instead of buying new ones.[9]

In addition to the basic U.S. economic indicators, our Serv-Pro tracks a number of key economic statistics for their marketing area and for the supermarket industry through their trade association and the Supermarket Institute. Because the company saw the "downshifting" of customer purchase patterns that preceded the 2008–2009 recession, the company postponed a warehouse expansion and, with a strong balance sheet and excellent inventory controls, was able to ride out the recession.

Here is the economic question for your councils: *What economic indicators should we review and begin monitoring for our markets and industry?*

Global Factors

Thomas Friedman, in his best-selling book *The World Is Flat*, describes the global trends that have knocked down barriers to trade and, with the advances of the digital revolution, made it possible to do business instantaneously across the globe. Friedman demonstrates that small firms, as well as large, are participating in this revolution.[10]

As with the other trends we have discussed, globalization creates a myriad of both threats and opportunities for companies. While it is easier now for a small business in the United States to pursue international markets, it is also easier for foreign enterprises to enter the domestic market, creating new competition. A case in point is Craftmaster, which assembles upholstered sofas and chairs in its plant in North Carolina. China-based Samson Holding Ltd. acquired Craftmaster to give their Chinese furniture subsidiary access to the U.S. market and to overcome the shipping and inventory issues associated with bulky sofas. The Chinese operation supplies Craftmaster with fabric, wooden frames, and other parts. Craftmaster handles the assembly, distribution, and marketing. Because of its low cost structure and strong financial backing, Craftmaster has gained significant market share, even during the grueling 2008–2009 recession, as other companies went out of business.[11] Conversely, Boggs & Partners Architects, based in Annapolis, Maryland, landed contracts in India, Qatar, and Bahrain and expects to generate as much as 90% of its revenue outside the United States in the next few years.[12]

As for our specialty food distributor, the company purchasing staff has regular video conferences with small food manufacturers in countries such as France and Italy to develop proprietary products for import and distribution exclusively to their customers' stores.

We are indeed in a "flat world," and you need to consider the opportunities and risks for your business. I suggest you read Friedman's book and then ask your advisory teams to consider the following question: *How will we compete in a flat world?*

Your Industry

Given our exploration of the general environment, we now turn to industry analysis. An industry, by definition, contains a group of companies offering products or services that relate to the same customer needs. For example, a variety of nonalcoholic carbonated beverages, fruit juices, and flavors of bottled water can all serve the same consumer need for refreshment. The companies that serve that need, such as Coca-Cola and PepsiCo, are in the *soft drink industry*. It is important to be clear about the boundaries of your industry; otherwise, new competitors with new products that may satisfy the same consumer needs may catch you by surprise. For example, Coca-Cola once thought of itself as being in the soda, or carbonated beverage, industry. The company was surprised in the 1990s when a rapid growth in consumer demand for bottled water and healthy juices began to cut into demand for sodas. Of course, Coca-Cola quickly responded with its own bottled water brand and acquisitions of juice makers, but still lost market share to PepsiCo, which was working from a broader industry definition and beat Coca-Cola to the market with noncarbonated drinks.[13]

Michael Porter, in his book *Competitive Advantage*, developed a framework for classifying and analyzing the characteristics of an industry's environment.[14] Porter recommends that businesses examine the following five forces that shape competition and influence the profit potential of any industry:

- Potential new entrants
- Bargaining power of buyers
- Bargaining power of suppliers
- Potential substitute products or services
- Rivalry among existing competitors

Each of these forces can be strong or weak in a given industry. A strong competitive force is a *threat* because it reduces profitability. A weak competitive force represents an *opportunity* because it allows a company to earn greater profits. You want to understand these forces so you can strategically position your business to succeed—defending against the threats and taking advantage of the opportunities. The analysis is also useful for assessing profit potential when you are thinking about entering a new industry. The five forces analysis lends itself well to working with your advisory groups, as you brainstorm on flip charts or whiteboard to identify elements under each of the forces that may affect your business. We will again use our specialty food distributor to illustrate application of the concepts as we briefly discuss each of the industry forces.

The Threat of New Entrants

How easy is it for new competitors to come into your industry? Are there potential competitors that may not be currently competing in your industry but have the capability to do so if they choose? By entering your industry, new competitors may take market share from you and your current competitors. Aided by rapidly changing technology, we are seeing more frequent industry crossovers: for example, cable companies offering traditional phone service, Internet drug companies dispensing prescriptions directly to consumers, Apple and Google entering the cell phone business, and Web-based news media supplanting newspapers.

A number of barriers regulate the threat of entry by new competitors. These barriers, such as economies of scale, switching costs, access to distribution channels, and government policy will vary from industry to industry. Table 2.1 provides a synopsis of these example barriers to entry and the implications for new entrants.

Here are some questions for your planning teams: *What new competitors might come into our marketplace? What barriers exist in our industry to deter new entrants? Strategically, which barriers can we develop or enhance to protect our business from new competition?*

Table 2.1. Example Barriers to Entry

Barrier description	Implications for potential competitors
Economies of scale: Firm has lower unit costs as the business increases in size and benefits from production efficiencies, spreading of fixed costs, and greater purchasing power.	A new company that enters the industry on a small scale may have a significant cost disadvantage or need additional financial investment to scale the operation to competitive size.
Switching costs: Customers will incur substantial time, people power, and money to switch to a new supplier.	Competitors have to offer customers significant incentives and hand-holding to acclimate them to change, reducing profits.
Access to distribution channels: Existing distribution channels are limited for new entrants due to established relationships or exclusivity agreements.	A new entrant will have to incur costs to develop new distribution channels.
Government policy: Regulations may require licenses or permits to conduct business.	Policies may make entry more difficult and costly; excessive government regulations may reduce profit potential.

Our specialty food distributor faced an unexpected example of competition from a new entrant during the dot-com boom in the late 1990s. Internet-based grocery distribution firms such as WebVan, financed by venture capitalists and public stock offerings, began building giant distribution centers and home delivery systems designed to bypass the traditional supermarket. Fortunately for our distributor, the home delivery concept failed to achieve critical mass and proved too costly, bankrupting the new competition.

On the plus side, Serv-Pro continually works to enhance two of the barriers to entry in its market segment. The first is switching costs. The company has worked diligently to seamlessly integrate its computer systems with its supermarket customers, providing, for example, electronic communication of product and pricing information tailored to the needs of each account. Over the years, the systems have become so dependable and intertwined that most customers would hesitate to change to a new supplier because of the time investment and potential risk of disrupting ongoing operations.

The second barrier employed by the distributor is access to distribution. The distributor has a number of agreements with specialty food manufacturers that give Serv-Pro the exclusive right to distribute and service certain product lines in the distributor's marketing area. In addition, the distributor has created several proprietary brands and imported product labels that have developed a loyal consumer following that would not be available to new entrants.

The Bargaining Power of Buyers

Buyers in a position to bargain can push down your prices and raise your expenses by demanding higher quality and more costly services. Conversely, buyers in a weak bargaining position enable industry companies to raise prices and improve profits. Buyers or customers in an industry tend to be more powerful when the following factors are in place:

- They buy in large quantities.
- They are few in number, and there are many sellers.
- The selling firm is dependent on the buyers for a significant portion of its revenue.

- Switching costs are low so the buyer can play off sellers against each other to force down prices.
- Buyers are in the position to produce the product themselves or buy directly from the manufacturer.

You can see these factors play out in favor of the buyer in many industries. For example, the auto component industry has many small suppliers attempting to serve just a few large automobile manufacturers, such as Ford and Toyota. Every point in the above bullet list applies, so it is no surprise that manufacturing automobile components is a tough business with meager profitability.

Here are two simple planning questions: *What type of bargaining power do your customers have? What can you do about it?* Our specialty food distributor struggles with those questions. The supermarket industry is notoriously low margin and is traditionally very aggressive in bargaining. The purchasing staff constantly holds the possibility of "going direct" over the heads of distributors or threatens to reduce space allocation in their stores if a supplier does not meet their demands for lower prices or additional services. Distributors often face demands for supplying additional personnel (i.e., free labor) at store openings and remodels. The best solution, one that most small businesses learn only after bitter experience, is *never let one account become too large a portion of your business.* For this reason, Serv-Pro avoids national chains and works, through consistent new business development, to keep any regional chain from exceeding 15% of their business.

Bargaining Power of Suppliers

Powerful suppliers mirror the implications of powerful customers. A supplier in a position of power has the ability to raise the price of raw materials and other inputs, such as products and services. A powerful supplier can also raise your costs by providing poor quality or service. Alternatively, if a supplier is weak, you may be able to bargain down prices or demand higher quality. Suppliers tend to be powerful when the following are true:

- There are only a few large suppliers, and the buyers are many and small.
- The suppliers' goods and services are essential to the buyer's success.

- The suppliers' products are unique, and substitute products are not available to the buying firm.
- The suppliers pose a credible threat to supply goods and services directly to the buyers' customers.

As with the bargaining power of buyers, you can see the power (and profits) of suppliers displayed in certain industries. For example, in the electronic game industry, Electronic Arts (EA) has power as a developer and supplier of games. Because of the quality of their games, Sony, Nintendo, and Microsoft are willing to pay a premium to contract for EA's products. Another example is Intel, which controls the bulk of the market for microprocessors and earns substantial profits as a result.

Serv-Pro has good fortune in terms of the supplier equation. The suppliers are primarily small manufacturers of specialized products who cannot afford to create direct consumer demand through advertising. Therefore, the suppliers are dependent on the distributor for wide distribution. In addition, on the retail side, the complexity of the product lines is so great that the distributor is given great leeway by the retailer in determining product selection, giving the distributor leverage with the supplier through the threat of deletion or reduced distribution. Use these two planning questions to think about supplier leverage in your industry: *What is your leverage with your suppliers? How can you increase your bargaining power as buyer?*

The Threat of Substitute Products or Services

Substitute products are goods and services that satisfy a buyer's needs in a different way. Think, for example, how mobile phones like the iPhone and the BlackBerry are becoming substitutes for laptop computers for business travelers, or how, when coffee prices rise, people may switch to tea or soft drinks. Video conferencing substituting for air travel is another example. As with other threats, substitution limits the prices that firms can charge. On the other hand, when there are few or no substitutes, firms have an opportunity to operate with higher prices and earn additional profits. Our country's perpetual battle with oil prices is an obvious example.

Consider the products or services that you provide. Here are some questions to think about: *Are there other ways for buyers to meet their needs? What can you do to lower the attractiveness of substitute products?*

Serv-Pro often competes with alternative or substitute supply chain approaches. For example, one chain decided to buy as many specialty food products as they could directly from the manufacturer, deliver them to the stores through their own grocery trucks, and require in-store labor to provide the detailed merchandising services required by the category. While the cost of product may be lower, such a method often results in lower sales and excess inventories. It is up to the specialty distributor to make a financial case for the value that their dedicated system provides as measured by shopper satisfaction and return on investment. One way to reduce the attractiveness of substitute products is to document the value of differentiated services or, in the case of products, the benefits of unique features not shared by the substitute.

Rivalry Among Existing Firms

Competitive rivalry is the set of actions and reactions between competitors as they compete for market position. The intensity of the rivalry influences prices as well as the costs of competing in such areas as facilities, product development, advertising, and sales costs. Some industries are characterized by very intense competitive rivalry because of such factors as low degree of differentiation, low switching costs for the buyers, and similar-sized competitors. The airline industry provides a good example of intense rivalry. For example, when one airline offers lower fares on a route, competitors flying the same route are quick to respond to match or beat the fares. In context of the five forces analysis, it is easy to understand why "running an airline is one of the more reliable ways to lose money."[15]

In other industries, where certain factors such as government regulations or patents constrain competition, rivalry may be less intense. The pharmaceutical industry is one example. Planning questions related to rivalry include the following: *How intense is the rivalry in your industry? How many competitors are there? Which competitors are most likely to respond to a specific competitive move?*

Serv-Pro experiences only a moderate degree of competitive rivalry in their marketing area. They compete directly with two national firms, which tend to focus on the national food chains; one regional distributor; and one local rival, a smaller company that specializes in ethnic foods. Supermarket chains like to "keep their suppliers honest" by allowing a competitor to service selected "test" stores, so Serv-Pro periodically has to respond to challenges by its competitors. However, given the barrier of switching costs and the differentiation in service quality, localized product variety, and long-term customer relationships with the regional operators, Serv-Pro has been able to moderate competitive intensity.

Direct Competitors

The last step in your study of the external environment is conducting a detailed analysis of each direct competitor. You want to understand each competitor's strategic intent and major strengths and weaknesses. Bradford and Duncan, in their book *Simplified Strategic Planning*, provide a good summary of the rationale for competitor analysis:

> You need to have a good understanding of what your competitors are up to—not so you can copy them (a common mistake), but so you can find a way to be different. The idea is to give your customers a reason other than low price for choosing to do business with you. . . . If you know a competitor's strengths and weaknesses, you can figure out a way to position yourself to avoid those strengths and take advantage of those weaknesses.[16]

You gain this intelligence about your competitors from a variety of sources, including observations in the field, conversations with vendors, Dun & Bradstreet credit reports, trade journals, trade association meetings, and Web sites. Teach your employees to pay attention to competitive activity and report anything they learn about a competitor. Use the information to create a profile on each competitor, and update the profile regularly as new information comes in. Table 2.2 provides a sample list of competitive information that can be important to the development of your strategic plan.

Table 2.2. Example Information From a Competitive Analysis

• Headquarters location	• Financial data
• Ownership	○ Sales volume/growth
• Profiles of senior leadership	○ Access to capital
• Vision/mission	○ Financial ratios
• Competitive strategy	• Number of employees
• Unique features and benefits of products or services	• Competitive strengths
• Target markets	• Competitive weaknesses
	• Significant recent events

Here is an example of the value of the competitor analysis process. Through competitor analysis, Serv-Pro found a weakness with one of their national competitors that provided an opportunity to enhance a competitive advantage. The national firm was experiencing excessive turnover of retail service employees, the specialists who stock, maintain, and order product. The national firm revised its compensation system to pay a straight percentage on the sales of product handled by each service person, attempting to stem the turnover by providing opportunity for higher income (and hopefully motivating service employees to work harder).

Serv-Pro has a different philosophy, believing their experienced retail service staff, with extensive product knowledge and advanced merchandising skills, are professionals who serve as a differentiator. The distributor has long paid an above average base salary, with good benefits, and offered a unique bonus plan that rewards service personnel for excellent performance in a variety of measures that are important to the customer, such as inventory control. Serv-Pro determined, as part of its strategic plan, to attack the competitor's weakness by further enhancing its service staff advantage. They developed a more systematic process for recruiting and selecting new hires and provided a more extensive training program that incorporated the latest Web-based learning tools. Serv-Pro also knew that paying service personnel on a commission basis increased the incentive to overstock customers. They used this knowledge to great advantage both to defend their current accounts and to gain entry to the competitor's accounts by documenting the excess inventory buildup in stores serviced by their competitor's commissioned salespeople.

In summary, the starting point of strategy formulation is an analysis of the forces that shape competition. The goal of the analysis is to gain an understanding of the opportunities and threats confronting your business so you can develop a strategy to take advantage of the opportunities and minimize the threats. The next step in strategy formulation is to think through your company's internal strengths and weaknesses. Chapter 3 will provide some useful ideas for making that analysis.

CHAPTER 3

Internal Analysis

To develop the best strategy, you need to understand your company's internal strengths and weaknesses in context of your mission. As part of your strategic plan, you want to build on those strengths that offer the best opportunity to gain advantage against your competitors and address any significant weaknesses that will hinder the accomplishment of your mission. Given your limited resources as a small business, you should focus your attention on the "critical few" improvements that will give you the greatest return. As part of the internal analysis, you also need to think about your financial condition and access to capital. In this chapter, we will look first at analyzing your business from an activity-based perspective and conclude by highlighting the financial issues.

Thinking About the Internal Structure of Your Business

A useful way to facilitate discussion of the internal strengths and weaknesses is simply to examine in some detail the activities in each of the functional areas of your business. As shown in Figure 3.1, most businesses organize around two fundamental functions: operations and support, with activity centers (sometimes called departments) within each functional area.[1]

The operational activities are involved directly in the physical creation of the product or service. Operational activities typically follow a process flow of inputs to outputs. Each stage in the process not only adds cost but also (we hope) creates value in the eyes of the customer. The support activities, as the name indicates, help enable and sustain the operational activities.

Here are some of the typical subactivities performed within each of the operational activity centers:[2]

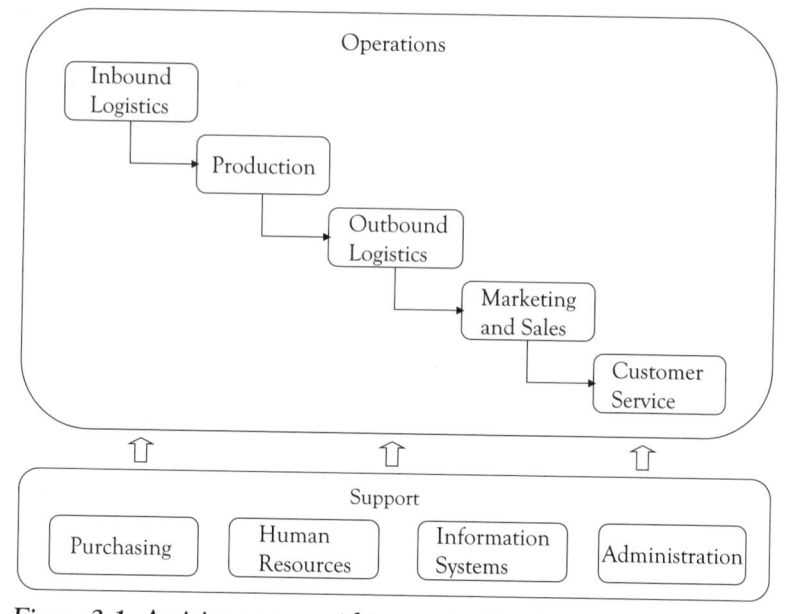

Figure 3.1. Activity centers within a typical business structure.

- *Inbound logistics.* Receiving, storing, and distributing inputs to the production process, including such activities as materials handling, inventory control, vehicle scheduling, and returns to suppliers
- *Production.* Transforming inputs into the final product form, including, in the case of manufacturing, machining, assembly, packaging, and equipment maintenance; in the case of services, such as retail or banking, providing the service to the customer
- *Outbound logistics.* Storing and distributing the product to buyers, including such activities as finished goods warehousing, material handling, order processing, scheduling, and delivery
- *Marketing and sales.* Providing buyers a means to purchase the product or service and convincing them to do so, such as channel selection, advertising, promotion, sales detailing, and pricing
- *Customer service.* Providing service to enhance or maintain the value of the product, such as installation, repair, training, parts supply, and performance guarantees

Support activities also play a vital role in the success of any business. Each support component can involve a wide range of distinct activities, often serving various operational activities across the firm. Examples include the following:

- *Purchasing.* Purchasing raw materials, services, supplies, and physical assets
- *Information systems.* Researching, acquiring or developing, and applying information technology across the organization, such as the use of computers and the Internet
- *Human resources.* Recruiting, hiring, training, and compensating personnel
- *Administration.* Financing, accounting, legal and government affairs, and quality control

Many manufacturing firms and service businesses will also have a separate function devoted to research and development for new products or services. Building capability for innovation can be a source of competitive advantage.[3]

It is easy to see how strengths or weaknesses in the support categories can affect the cost of doing business, important competitive factors such as customer satisfaction, or both. Improved purchasing practices, for example, can improve the cost or quality of inputs, thereby lowering other costs across the business, from receiving to after-sale returns. Technology that automates the process of order entry can reduce errors and improve customer service. Improving recruiting and hiring practices can reduce employee turnover, thereby reducing turnover-related costs in the primary activities. Even administration, sometimes viewed as "overhead," can provide powerful sources of competitive advantage. For example, effective accounting information systems that provide timely information in a decision-making format can lead to better decisions that reduce costs or improve customer service.

Your task is to study each activity area in detail, determine the activities important to your mission, and then figure out ways to do things better, faster, and at lower cost and/or to perform the activity in a way that better meets buyer needs and, therefore, contributes to differentiation from your competition.

One of the best ways to identify your company's relevant strengths and weaknesses is to ask your employees, especially those on the front line of the business. They know. You may want to expand your existing employee advisory team for the internal analysis to make sure you have a representative sample of your best thinkers from all the functional areas, especially those who are in touch with the customer.

Analyzing the Activities in Your Business

So how do you conduct the internal activity analysis? You assemble your team in a room with flip charts and systematically talk through the structure and activities of your business, cataloging your significant subactivities under major activity centers or departmental headings. Capture everything your firm does in an operational or supporting category. But do not get too detailed here. Employee training, for example, is a sufficient description of a major subactivity. There is no need to list all the different types of training you deliver in your organization. Again, you are looking to identify activities that have a high potential impact on differentiation, that represent a significant or growing portion of your cost, or both.

You also want to think about the linkages within the operational and support functions. Businesses are not a collection of independent activities but a system of *interdependent* activities. Linkages are relationships between the way one value activity is performed and the cost or performance of another. For example, in a steel fabrication shop, purchasing high-quality, precut steel sheets can simplify the manufacturing process and reduce the cost of scrap. In a restaurant, the use of labor-scheduling software can improve staffing during peak times, which not only improves customer satisfaction but also capacity utilization (table turnover). A change in the receiving process can improve inventory accuracy, reducing order-processing costs downstream. Sometimes the linkages are difficult to recognize, but the ability to do so can yield a sustainable source of competitive advantage.

To help illustrate the process, Figure 3.2 provides an example of selected items from Serv-Pro's activity analysis. The chart identifies activities the strategic planning team felt were key to Serv-Pro's mission. Once you have your lists of subactivities and discuss the linkages, you can

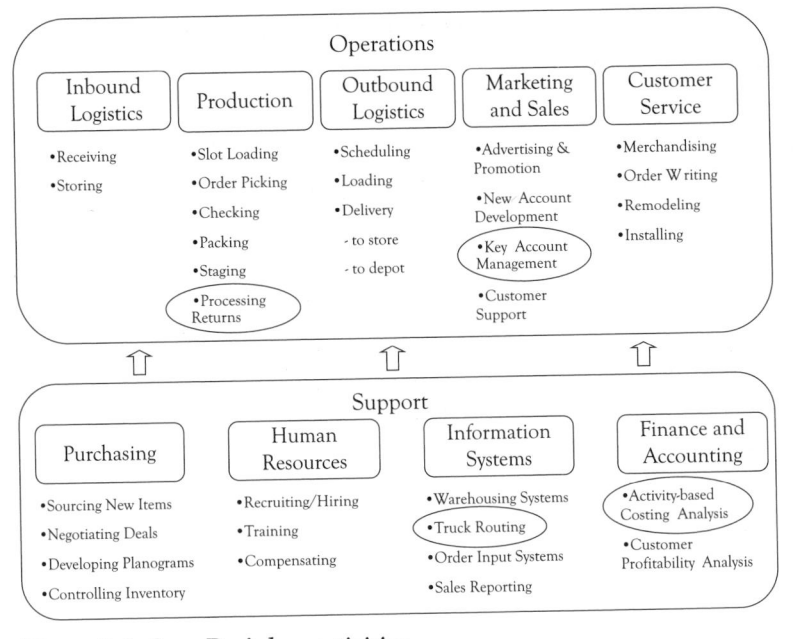

Figure 3.2. Serv-Pro's key activities.

debate where the strengths and weaknesses lie in context of your mission. Look for consensus on the few key areas of opportunity that could help further differentiate your company from the competition or significantly improve your cost structure. The Serv-Pro planning team determined four key areas of opportunity that should become the focus of strategic initiatives (circled in Figure 3.2).

The selection of the key opportunities was the result of a ranking and rating system applied to each of the activity centers. Table 3.1 provides an example analysis from Serv-Pro's marketing and sales department. After listing the major subactivities under sales and marketing, the Serv-Pro team discussed and rated each activity on a 5-point scale on three dimensions: current impact on mission (weakness to strength), potential for differentiation (low to high), and potential for cost reduction (low to high). From the discussion and resulting ratings, it became clear that the activities related to key account management had strategic implications for the company. The team considered key account management a weakness but felt the activity had a high potential for differentiation from competitors and could have a potential positive impact on costs.

Table 3.1. Example Sales and Marketing Activity Analysis: Specialty Food Distributor

Sales and marketing Activities	Assessment of impact on mission			Potential for differentiation			Potential for cost reduction		
	Weakness		Strength	Low		High	Low		High
Advertising and promotion	1 2 ③ 4 5			1 2 ③ 4 5			① 2 3 4 5		
New account development	1 2 3 ④ 5			1 ② 3 4 5			① 2 3 4 5		
Key account management ☆	① 2 3 4 5			1 2 3 4 ⑤			1 2 3 ④ 5		
Customer support	1 2 3 ④ 5			1 2 3 ④ 5			1 ② 3 4 5		

To further illustrate the thinking process, let's look at Serv-Pro's rationale for selecting the four key strategic initiatives. We'll look in depth at the account manager issue and touch on the other three.

Key Account Management

For Serv-Pro, the key account management function had evolved to a major activity as the business grew more complex. As the company began to serve larger regional supermarket chains, it became necessary to assign an individual to the headquarters of each chain to serve as a liaison between the chain and the distributor. The account manager worked directly with the various chain functions, such as purchasing and merchandising, to coordinate new item introductions, retail prices, and promotions and to plan the distributor's role in store installations and remodels. Over time, the position expanded to include business development activities such as making presentations on new product categories and conducting business reviews. The account manager regularly interacted with all the distributor's functions to solve problems and coordinate initiatives for the particular chain he or she represented.

The team rated the key account management activity as a weakness because a number of chains had complained about the effectiveness of their account manager and his or her ability to deal with the demands of the job. The distributor's practice had been to promote individuals, usually supervisors from the field service organization who were considered great merchandisers, into the position. The problem was that most of the individuals did not have a "whole system" understanding of the other distributor functions, such as purchasing or warehouse operations, nor the education to deal with increasingly sophisticated customers who were asking, for example, for more financial and product performance analysis. As a point person for problems from both the distributor side and the customer side, the account manager also had to have extraordinary problem-solving and interpersonal communication skills. It was a tough job.

But the difficulty of the job and the value to the customer also created an opportunity for differentiation from competitors. As the daily interface with key decision makers at chain headquarters, the account manager was, in essence, the face of the company. A professional and effective account manager could positively influence customer relations and satisfaction and would represent the type of "human capital" that would be difficult for competitors to duplicate.

Account managers were also in a unique position to influence costs related to serving their assigned chain. The nature of a supermarket customer is one of constant demands to a direct store delivery vendor—more frequent deliveries, lower costs on promotions, more people assigned to store remodels, more product variety, lower inventories—the demands are endless. An account manager with strong negotiation skills can often mitigate the cost impact and create win–win solutions. In addition, with good selling skills, an account manager can increase space allocations, category expansion, and new item distribution, raising sales volume. Increasing the average order size per store can have a dramatic effect on distributor cost economics since there are a number of nonvariable costs associated with producing and delivering an order.

As you can see from the foregoing discussion, the account management activity was indeed worthy of strategic consideration for this distributor. As part of the strategic plan, the company determined to incorporate a strategic initiative focused on upgrading the account management function by improving recruiting, selecting, training, and support. The next chapter provides examples of how to execute such an initiative through tactical action planning.

Other Serv-Pro Activities Selected for Strategic Focus

In addition to the account manager opportunity, the Serv-Pro planning team decided to focus on three other activities: returns processing, truck routing, and activity-based costing.

Returns processing relates to the guaranteed sale function that is standard in Serv-Pro's industry. The guaranteed sales commitment requires the distributor to return for full credit slow selling, discontinued, or leftover promotional product from the customer. The current process is inefficient and costly and can tie up large amounts of capital in the processing queue.

The truck routing issue is also cost related, due to an expected expansion in geographic coverage, ongoing increases in gasoline prices, and the need to make sure trucks depart fully loaded ("cubed out"). It also has a customer service impact (timeliness and reliability) that could serve as a differentiator. Implementation of new sophisticated routing software may be part of the solution here.

Finally, activity-based costing is a strength the company would like to enhance and refine, believing the skill will become even more important in the future for controlling costs and in negotiating proposals with increasingly sophisticated customers.

In summary, note again the selectivity—a decision to focus on just a few activities with the intent of implementing strategic initiatives to improve significantly the activities to better support the mission of the business. The secret for a small business is always staying focused—concentrating your energy on the few things that will make the most difference and then following through.

Financial Considerations

As part of your internal analysis, you must understand the financial needs of your business and consider your access to capital. Inadequate cash flow can kill your business. Easy access to capital can provide a competitive advantage when opportunity knocks. Establishing good financial controls and arranging adequate financing to support a chosen strategy may seem obvious, but failure to think deeply about the financial perspective is often a stumbling block for small business owners and managers. While a detailed discussion of finances is beyond the scope of this book, the following are some questions to think through with your financial advisors as part of your internal analysis.[4]

1. *Do you have a good financial and information reporting system that provides timely reports?* You need cash flow statements, balance sheets, profit-and-loss statements, key financial ratios, and key performance indicators for your operational and support activities. These reports need to be in a decision-making format, providing history, trends, and comparisons against benchmarks or targets.

2. *Do you meet with your management team and key employees to review your performance reports on a scheduled basis?* There is a natural tendency for a small business owner/manager to keep the numbers "close to the vest." However, research indicates that an "open book" management strategy that educates and involves employees in financial decisions improves decision making and performance at all levels of an organization.[5]

3. *Do you understand the working capital needs of your business?* Working capital is the difference between a business's current assets (cash, inventory, and accounts receivable) and liabilities (accounts payable, short-term debt). As you grow, managing the working-capital cash-conversion cycle—the length of time between payment of what you owe and the collection of your receivables—is critical. For example, what is the impact on your cash flow if you decide to provide extended payment terms to a big, new customer as part of your competitive strategy? You must be able to answer this type of question.

4. *Do you know the capital needs for your business for the future?* If, for example, your strategy calls for geographic expansion and you will need to expand your production facilities or warehouse, how much money will you need? A common problem is to underestimate the investment. A new production facility may cost $10 million, but you may need another $2 million to cover startup expenses and other "soft" costs.

5. *What can you do to obtain access to capital?* When new business opportunities present themselves, where will you find the capital? There are two types of funding: equity and debt. Regarding equity,

you can invest your own money or bring in partners. Just remember that partners and equity investors bring other things to the table as well as money. On the positive side, partners can bring access to new customers or suppliers. On the negative side, partners may have different expectations in terms of growth, return on their investment, or the time frame for cashing out. Sources for debt financing fall into two basic categories: private sources, such as local banks, credit unions, or insurance companies, and public sources, such as the U.S. Small Business Administration. The point here is that you must be proactive, developing relationships with potential lenders and educating them on your strategy and your business *before* you need the money.

To this point in our review of the fundamentals of the strategic planning process, we have

- discussed the importance of vision and mission,
- walked through the process of conducting an external analysis of your environment to identify opportunities and threats,
- reviewed a method for conducting an internal analysis of your business to identify strengths and weaknesses.

Now we are ready to discuss the development of a strategic plan.

CHAPTER 4

Strategy

Your strategy describes your competitive game plan—how you are going to position your company in the marketplace to gain a sustainable, competitive advantage that will allow you to earn above-average rates of return on your investment. In this chapter, we will look at a simple model for thinking about your strategic options and examine some fundamental principles for developing a distinctive strategic position. The goal is to construct a clear strategy that everyone in your business can understand, internalize, and use as a framework for decision making in pursuit of your mission.

A Basic Model for Strategic Positioning

At the simplest level, two decision elements describe a firm's strategy: (a) the basis for competitive advantage and (b) the scope of the target market.[1] A company can obtain competitive advantage either through price or uniqueness in product or service and can seek to compete in either a broad or narrow market. As shown in Figure 4.1, the decision process results in four basic alternative strategic positions within an industry.

Each of these four alternative strategies involves a fundamentally different approach to competitive advantage. The broad price leadership strategy seeks to produce goods or services at the lowest cost and competes primarily on price, selling to the broadest market possible to gain volume and economies of scale. The differentiation strategy, also targeted to a broad market, seeks to be unique in its industry based on one or more dimensions that are widely valued by buyers and justify a premium price. The means of differentiation vary by industry but typically include such factors as product innovation, technological capability, superior quality, or exceptional customer service. The focused versions of these strategies use the price or uniqueness advantage in

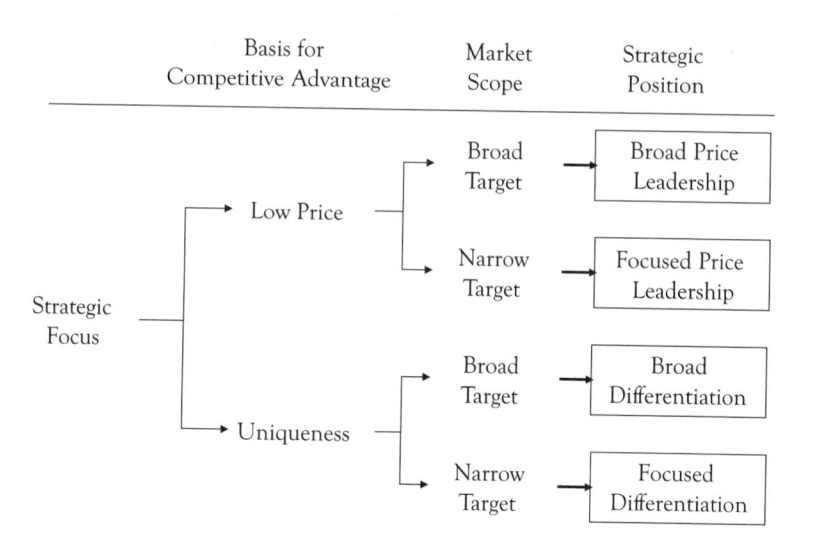

Figure 4.1. Basic alternative strategic positions.

narrower market segments, targeting selected groups of customers with similar needs.

To illustrate how the four basic strategies naturally manifest themselves in a competitive environment, it is interesting to think about examples within various industries. For example, in the supermarket industry, it is easy to identify chains that have taken different strategic positions. Wal-Mart definitely provides price leadership for a broad segment of consumers. Aldi, the German-owned food chain rapidly expanding in the United States, is positioned in the focused price leadership box, targeting a narrower segment of customers who are willing to accept mostly private label items, limited selection, and few amenities in return for rock-bottom prices (even lower than Wal-Mart). Florida-based grocer Publix, known for its exceptional customer service and attention to important customer factors such as cleanliness, exemplifies a broad differentiation strategy. Finally, Trader Joe's exemplifies the focused differentiation position, catering to upscale customers who value a wide selection of exotic, natural, and organic foods, many of which are unique private labels.

Based on this model, your first strategic decision is to determine which box you want to play in. Good strategic planning requires you to make a choice. It is very difficult to engage in multiple strategic positions, especially for a small business. A firm that attempts "to be all things to all people" has no strategy. The firm will be caught in the inherent contradictions and tradeoffs of different strategies and will compete at a disadvantage with more focused firms. Here is the mantra for the small businessperson that is the theme of this book: Be focused, be different, and be better. Consistent with your financial position and access to capital, select your niche and determine to dominate. For most small businesses, the focused differentiation strategy, tailored to a specific market segment, makes the most sense and is the best path to profitability and personal satisfaction.

Principles of Strategic Positioning

Given the basic model for strategic positioning, we now need to review six fundamental principles for establishing and maintaining a distinctive competitive advantage within your chosen box.[2] To help illustrate each principle, we will consider two businesses that pursue the focused differentiation strategy: a manufacturing firm, Tervis Tumbler Company,[3] and a service business, Cat Care of Fayette.[4] Tervis Tumbler, headquartered in North Venice, Florida, manufactures crystal-clear insulated drinkware sold through wholesale and retail channels. Cat Care is a successful veterinary care clinic based in Fayetteville, Georgia. Both companies demonstrate how a strong competitive advantage comes from the application of strategic-positioning principles.

Here are the six principles:

1. *You must begin with the right goals.* You want to achieve above-average financial performance (measured by return on equity), maintain customer satisfaction, and engender employee commitment. You have to achieve all three goals to succeed. The wrong goals create trouble. For example, when you define your goals in terms of size or volume measures, such as market share, dysfunctional decisions often follow. This approach is a common problem for the small businessperson, who is tempted to go after any customer, match any competitor's price, and add any product line or service in the pursuit of volume and growth. Over time, costs go up, complexity increases, service declines, and the firm finds itself with financial difficulties, unhappy customers, and discouraged employees.

Examples:

According to Laura Spencer, CEO of Tervis, the company mantra is "profitable" growth. The company has experienced steady sales increases by concentrating on specialty retailers, the corporate gift market, and sports licenses. Spencer notes that the company could easily "cheapen the product" and sell to mass-market retailers, but the company prefers to "control its own destiny." Tervis ties performance metrics to initiatives that improve product quality, production efficiency, and employee morale and productivity.

Rather than focus solely on growth, Dr. Lori Stearns, Cat Care owner and senior veterinarian, focuses her business goals around "developing a more intimate relationship with clients." According to Stearns, "We could grow our business by adding more doctors, but I find we prosper by doing what we love and living a balanced life. When we limit the number of clients we book in a day and spend more time with each client, our revenue per client and client referrals actually increase."

2. *You must deliver a meaningful value proposition.* A company's strategy must deliver a set of customer benefits that are different from your competitor's. Remember that benefits describe how your product or service meets a customer's needs or purchase criteria. You must be able to explain to a customer why he or she should buy from you rather than a competitor.

Examples:

Laura Spencer describes Tervis's value proposition succinctly with three words: "customization, rapid delivery, and durability." Tervis tumblers, with unique designs or logos inserted between the two walls of the insulated product, are built to order. Tervis's efficient production process, which takes place in a U.S.-based plant, allows quick response time to customer orders. Competitive tumblers are manufactured in Asia and are plagued with all the delivery problems associated with a long supply chain. The company builds a premium product that is so durable it is backed by a lifetime guarantee. If a tumbler ever cracks or leaks, the company replaces the tumbler free.

Dr. Stearns positions Cat Care as "catering only to felines and small furry exotics, such as rabbits, gerbils, and hamsters that have a similar physiology to cats." Cat Care's value proposition focuses on pet owners who desire a comprehensive range of personal, state-of-the-art health care services in an environment tailored exclusively for their cat or small furry animal. According to Stearns, "Cats do much better in their preferred environment and research proves they spend less time recovering from illness or injury."

3. *You must create a distinctive set of operational and support activities, and link the activities.* An effective strategy depends on identifying a distinctive set of activities within your business that support your value proposition. You have to perform activities tailored to your strategy that are different from those of your rivals or perform similar activities in a different way. In addition, you have to link your business activities in such a way that they are mutually reinforcing. Product design for a manufacturer, for example, should enhance the efficiency of the production process and reduce the need for after-sales service. Such interdependent fit makes your strategy harder to imitate. Competitors may easily copy one activity but will have greater difficulty duplicating a completely interconnected system. Sustainability of competitive advantage comes from the activity system, not the parts.

Examples:

Two engineers invented the Tervis Tumbler in 1946 and the product has undergone over 60 years of continuous improvement. While the company has unique expertise in plastics and a modern, lean manufacturing system, Laura Spencer notes the design and production process required to produce a tumbler that never cracks or leaks is a "combination of art and science," which is very hard to duplicate. On the marketing side, Tervis has a large number of licenses with both collegiate and professional sports teams that give the company a competitive edge.

Cat Care offers a comprehensive array of services including annual exams, boarding, dental cleaning, grooming, neutering, surgery, in-house laboratory, medications, pet care supplies, and prescription diet foods that are all feline specific. Their veterinarians are feline specialists, the medical equipment is feline friendly, the grooming and spa services are feline focused, and their playrooms and boarding facilities are designed exclusively for cats and small furry exotics. All the activities in the clinic relate and reinforce one another in support of Cat Care's strategy and value proposition.

4. *You must be prepared to make tradeoffs.* The nature of strategy requires tradeoffs and hard choices. For example, if you base your value proposition on offering the lowest prices, you will not be able to compete on fashion or variety. You may have to forgo some product features, services, or activities in order to spend time and money to become unique in others. The tradeoffs you make are what distinguish you strategically from other firms.

Examples:

Laura Spencer sees one of her roles as CEO at Tervis is to keep the company focused. For example, avoiding the mass-market retailers is a classic tradeoff, giving up volume for prestige and profitability. Limiting variety in their product line in order to focus on quality and efficiency is another tradeoff decision.

As a "no dog allowed" establishment, the tradeoffs for Cat Care are clear. Customers who own both cats and dogs have to choose to go to another veterinarian, or they have to subdivide their veterinary services, using more than one clinic. While many customers choose the latter, some customers are lost to competing veterinarians due to the inconvenience.

5. *You must maintain continuity.* Successful strategy requires continuity of direction. You must stay true to your positioning, even if that means passing up certain opportunities. Without continuity of direction, it is difficult to develop essential knowledge and skills or build a strong reputation in the marketplace. Frequent "reinvention" of the company reflects poor strategic thinking and is a route to high costs and mediocrity. The Hay Group consulting firm, in conducting research for *Fortune* magazine's Most Admired Companies listing, found that a strong, stable strategy was the most important contributing factor to the sterling reputations of the listed companies.[5]

Examples:

As noted earlier, Tervis has stayed true to its roots for over 60 years. Laura Spencer notes that the company has turned down a number of opportunities to apply their expertise to other plastic products. The company has chosen instead to diversify the channels of distribution for their core product in order to continue their steady growth. Their business channels now include wholesale, corporate gift and promotional giveaways, sports (e.g., golf and tennis), the Internet, and a limited number of company-owned retail stores.

Cat Care has remained consistent with their strategy since their opening in 2003. Their laser focus on cats translates into a strong reputation and credibility in the community as "cat experts."

6. *You must attend to operational effectiveness.* Executing business fundamentals, maintaining operational excellence, and performing similar activities more efficiently than rivals must work in tandem with strategic positioning. Continually reducing average unit costs represents the "table stakes" necessary to play in almost any industry today. You should aggressively pursue all cost-reduction opportunities that do not negatively affect your differentiating activities.

Examples:

To reduce costs, Tervis has invested heavily in a new factory, featuring lean manufacturing systems and an order-processing system that integrates all functions. The company tracks daily metrics for each manufacturing cell and regularly meets with employees to discuss ideas for continuous improvement.

Cat Care's focused strategy also facilitates their tight control on costs. If Cat Care were to choose to treat other animals, it would reduce their efficiencies. Their technicians and reception staff would need additional training. The clinic would need to purchase additional medical equipment, build separate boarding facilities, acquire more land for dog walking, and increase their inventory of pharmaceuticals.

Serv-Pro's Example of Strategic Positioning

Our specialty foods distributor, Serv-Pro, can provide us with a final example of strategic positioning, with particular emphasis on the fit of activities that provide both competitive advantage and sustainability. As part of its ongoing strategic review, the company seeks to refine its uniqueness and strengthen the fit and interdependence among its activities. As a reminder, here are the company's vision and mission statements:

Vision: to surprise and delight the supermarket shopper with the best variety of creatively merchandised specialty food products, creating happy retailers and satisfied stakeholders.

Mission: to satisfy the specialty and gourmet food needs of the supermarket shopper while improving the return on invested capital and space for our retail supermarket customers in the New England states. We meet the needs of our shoppers and our retailers through innovative logistical and supply-chain solutions and customized retail merchandising services.

Serv-Pro's strategy is *focused differentiation*. Their customer focus is on regional supermarket chains and independent food stores in their marketing area. They do very little business with national supermarket or discount chains, preferring to "work closely with local operators at the headquarters level." The company bases its differentiation on three related services:

1. Offering an inventory selection that features significant product depth and breadth across all specialty food categories tailored to the local market
2. Designing innovative, customized logistics solutions for major customers
3. Providing exceptional execution of merchandising services at the retail level

Following the principles of strategic positioning, the company is careful to focus on the right metrics related to financial performance, customer satisfaction, and employee morale and productivity. To grow the business at a controlled pace, Serv-Pro seeks to penetrate more retailers within their existing territory and increase the average order size with current customers. They do not seek growth for growth's sake. We will look more at Serv-Pro's "balanced scorecard" in the next chapter when we discuss success measures.

Serv-Pro's value proposition is contained within their mission statement. Successful retailers value two things: satisfied shoppers and productivity of their capital and space, which leads to a higher return on investment. So greater shopper satisfaction and return on investment is what Serv-Pro is really selling, not product or price. Understanding this principle is crucial in helping the company develop new business and defend their existing business.

Making their value chain activities more distinctive and interdependent is Serv-Pro's current strategic interest. Their external analysis reinforced the threat of the bargaining power of buyers, as their current customers continue to grow larger and acquisitions of regional chains by national and international operators become more prevalent. Their internal analysis identified some weaknesses that needed attention, as well as some strengths that could be enhanced to give the company greater differentiation from competitors and better bargaining power with retailers.

Activity-system maps are a useful tool for visualizing how a company executes its strategic position through a set of tailored value chain activities.[6] Figure 4.2 illustrates how Serv-Pro's activities connect to deliver competitive advantage. The company implements the higher order strategic themes (circles) through clusters of tightly linked activities (rectangles). For example, a complex web of activities and systems supports the theme of inventory depth and breadth (left circle in the diagram). The activities, all linked through interactive online computer systems, include purchasing, deal buying, receiving, promotional planning, and communication to the field through electronic planograms and the account managers. The connected system has taken years to develop, works smoothly, and would be very difficult to duplicate. The dotted line boxes, based on Serv-Pro's internal analysis, represent the target areas for improvement in the current strategic plan.

To emphasize a key point, the objective is to perform activities tailored to your strategy that are different from those of rivals or to perform

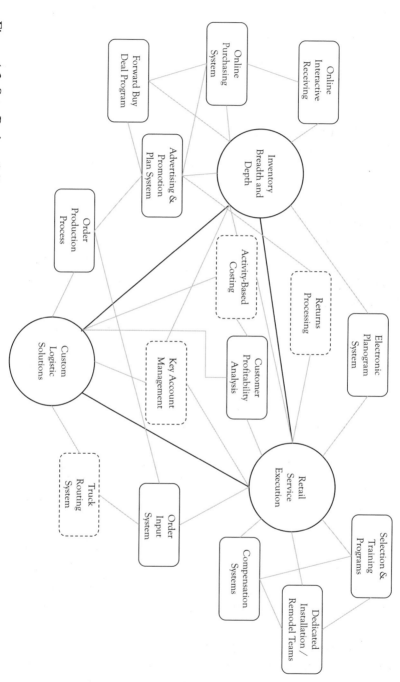

Figure 4.2. Serv-Pro's activity-system map.

Online Interactive Receiving

Online Purchasing System

Forward Buy Deal Program

Advertising & Promotion Plan System

Inventory Breadth and Depth

Order Production Process

Activity-Based Costing

Returns Processing

Electronic Planogram System

Custom Logistic Solutions

Key Account Management

Customer Profitability Analysis

Retail Service Execution

Truck Routing System

Order Input System

Compensation Systems

Dedicated Installation / Remodel Teams

Selection & Training Programs

similar activities in a distinctive way. In addition, you want to link your value chain activities, as illustrated by the diagram, in such a way that they are mutually reinforcing and difficult to duplicate by your competitors. Remember: Strategy, in the final analysis, rests on deliberately choosing a unique set of activities to deliver differentiated value. How the activities fit together drives both competitive advantage and sustainability.

Activity-system maps can also be useful for examining and strengthening strategic fit. Here are some questions to think about as you develop your activity maps:[7]

- Is each activity consistent with the overall strategic positioning?
- Can those responsible for each activity identify how other activities within the company improve or detract from their performance?
- Are there ways to strengthen how activities and groups of activities reinforce one another?
- Could changes in one activity eliminate the need to perform others?

Tradeoffs and hard choices are an integral part of Serv-Pro's strategic process. Their tight focus on a relatively narrow product line (specialty foods), customer segment (regional supermarkets), and geography (New England states) means they periodically pass on volume-enhancing opportunities. They do not do this reflexively, but carefully study each opportunity for strategic fit. For example, a general merchandise distributor in their area filed for bankruptcy, and a customer asked Serv-Pro to consider adding the failed distributor's product lines. While the products, such as pet supplies and electrical devices, had some similar handling characteristics, the company decided not to pursue the business because they felt it would distract from their core competence and create problems with their warehousing and logistical systems.

An even harder choice presented itself when a national discount chain, entering the New England area, approached Serv-Pro because of their premier reputation and asked for a proposal for distributing certain lines of specialty foods. After numerous meetings and even a trip to the chain's national headquarters, Serv-Pro declined to bid for the business for two reasons: the complexity and expense of meeting the chain's information system requirements and a reluctance to deal with the chain's bargaining power and reputation for squeezing small vendors.

On the other hand, Serv-Pro recently expanded into selected refrigerated and frozen specialty food items, a significant cost investment, but one the company felt was congruent with their core business, customer needs, and strategic position. In particular, the level of expertise and complexity required to manage the new product lines represented another opportunity for differentiation and could further raise switching costs for customers.

As the discussion on tradeoffs illustrates, the best way for most small businesses to grow profitably is to concentrate on deepening a strategic position rather than broadening and compromising it. A leader must define and communicate the company's unique position, forge fit among its activities, and have the courage to make the necessary tradeoffs.

Given the development of a strategy, in the next chapter we will look at the tactical aspects of putting a strategic plan into action using focused initiatives and action plans. We will also discuss ways to track and measure success.

CHAPTER 5

Tactics

In this chapter, we will consider the tactical aspects of translating your strategy into concrete actions to move your company forward. At this point, you have articulated a vision and mission, examined your external environment for opportunities and threats, analyzed your internal activities for strengths and weaknesses, and clarified your strategy. You should have a good idea of what you need to do to move your strategy forward. The problem is, your team is already working more than full time on the day-to-day aspects of the business, and your scarcest resource is the productive time of your key people. Strategic initiatives are future oriented and represent extra work and time. It is very easy to become sidetracked by the "tyranny of the urgent" if there is no system to keep everyone's attention on the long-term agenda.

As we discussed in previous chapters, the first key for effective follow-up is focus. Selecting just a few initiatives—the ones that will have the greatest impact—acknowledges the reality of limited resources, especially time, and increases the odds of accomplishment. The second key is to use two proven management tools that link to your strategy: action plan documents and a tracking system of success measures.

Creating Action Plans

You need to create an action plan document for each strategic initiative. The purpose of the action plan tool is to translate each strategic initiative into a series of tangible, manageable tasks with timelines and assigned responsibilities. To illustrate the process, Table 5.1 provides an action plan in its simplest form for our specialty food distributor. The strategic initiative focuses on improving one of Serv-Pro's value-chain activities: truck routing. Recalling the discussion in chapter 4, the truck-routing issue relates to a key strategic theme for the distributor: customized logistic

Table 5.1. Example Action Plan

Serv-Pro strategic action plan			
Strategic initiative	Upgrade truck-routing system		
Project objective	Implement a new truck-routing system that will reduce costs and improve customer service by May 20XX		
Team members	John (project leader), Carlos, Sarah, Keith, Song Joo		
Task	**Responsibility**	**Complete**	**Notes**
Clarify problem/identify needs			
• Identify current issues and problems	John w/ team	May 01	Include customer interviews
• Create "wish list" of capabilities	John w/ team	May 15	
Prepare request for proposal			
• List design/system requirements	Keith	Jun 15	
• Identify and schedule potential vendors	Sarah	Jun 30	Minimum 5 vendors
• Conduct preliminary meetings w/ vendors	John w/ team	Jul 15	90-minute meetings
• Prepare and send RFPs (requests for proposals) to top 3 vendors	Keith	Jul 30	
Select vendor proposal			
• Analyze vendor proposals	John w/ team	Sep 15	
• Prepare pro forma budget and cost/benefit analysis	Carlos	Oct 01	
• Review assumptions and budget	Team	Oct 15	Include all leadership
• Include approved funds in FY XX budget	Carlos	Nov 01	
• Select vendor and notify	John	Nov 15	
• Review and sign contract	John	Dec 15	
Install software			
• Create installation/communication plan	Song Joo	Jan 15	
• Install software application	Song Joo	Feb 15	
• Test software	John w/ team +	Mar 15	Target additional participants
• Conduct user training	Sarah	May 01	
• Complete implementation	Song Joo	May 15	
Evaluate			
• Create evaluation plan	Sarah	Jun 01	
• Review evaluation plan	Team		
• Conduct evaluation	Sarah		
• Review evaluation results	Team	Dec 01	Include all leadership

solutions. Truck routing also relates to operational efficiency and cost control, given an expected expansion in geographic coverage as customers build new stores, ongoing increases in gasoline prices, and the need to "cube out" trucks to reduce cost per mile. Routing also has a customer service impact (timeliness and reliability) that can be a differentiator.

Referring to the topical headings in Table 5.1, here are some tips to help you create an effective action plan document:

1. *Project objective.* Describe the project in terms of the intended outcome and indicate a target date for completion.
2. *Team members.* Remember the principle "people support what they help create." Ask those who will be involved in the execution of each initiative to help write the action plan. For efficiency, staff the project team with no more than five to seven primary members who represent the different functions affected by the project. Research indicates that teams with more than seven members experience significant loss in productivity and member satisfaction.[1] The truck-routing project, for example, should include representatives from outbound logistics, information systems, marketing, service, and accounting. The team leader should be a senior manager with good facilitation skills. The team can draw on additional expertise on an ad hoc basis when required.
3. *Task.* Start each action step with a strong verb–noun combination that is clear and specific ("test software," "conduct training"). A good way to develop the initial task list is for the team to brainstorm using index cards. A team member should serve as scribe and, using a bold marker, record verb–noun actions on individual index cards as the team members call out ideas. After creating a number of action cards, the team can spread the cards across the conference table and group them into categories of related activities. After some additional brainstorming, the team can sort the cards into categories and arrange them in a logical sequence for execution. A team member can then transcribe the cards into a worksheet similar to Table 5.1 for additional discussion and refinement at a subsequent meeting.
4. *Responsibility.* The team should assign each action step to an individual willing to accept responsibility for completing the action

according to the schedule. Each "action step owner" can involve others on the team or in the organization as required and should keep the team informed regarding problems or developments that might affect the schedule.

5. *Complete.* This column identifies the desired completion date for each action step, with all the dates building to the implementation date for the whole project. The team should be realistic in setting these dates, recognizing that all the team members are already busy with their full-time regular jobs, being conscious of the seasonal spikes in workload that occur in most businesses, and acknowledging that unexpected delays will surely occur. In other words, build a little slack into the schedule, but then stay committed to meeting the established deadlines.

6. *Notes.* Use this column to include special reminders or expectations agreed to by the team.

You can expand the action plan form shown in Table 5.1, of course, to include other columns as required to support the project. For example, some might prefer a start date column to go with the completion date to help clarify actions that the team can work on concurrently. You could replace the notes column, where appropriate, with a deliverables column that specifies a tangible outcome, such as a report or statistical analysis that must be delivered to the team at the conclusion of an action step. Finally, many action plans include a column for budget or dollars, to indicate the amount of money beyond normal budgets required to complete a particular action. For more sophisticated projects, software, such as Microsoft Project, is available to simplify the production and maintenance of the plan document.

Whatever the action plan format used, recognize the tool as an important part of your strategic controls as a senior leader. Every year, your company should be engaged in three or four strategic initiatives designed to improve your strategic position and competitive advantage. Assigning members to the project teams and meeting with your teams to review the status of each action plan on a regular basis represents one of the most important investments of your time.

Creating a Success Scorecard

In addition to closely managing your strategic initiatives, you also need a system of measures to focus everyone's attention on the important day-to-day drivers of your strategy. It is a fundamental management principle that what gets measured (and rewarded) is what gets done.[2] However, repeating a consistent theme in this book, keep the system of measurements simple, focusing on a short list of selected indicators that link directly to the success of your strategy. A number of studies have indicated that attempting to track too many performance measures can actually decrease performance.[3] One of the most practical tools for translating strategy into action through quantifiable objectives and measures is the balanced scorecard concept, developed by Kaplan and Norton (see Figure 5.1).[4]

The balanced scorecard complements traditional financial measures (which are the results of actions already taken) with criteria that measure performance from three additional strategic perspectives: customers, internal business processes, and learning—real-time operational measures

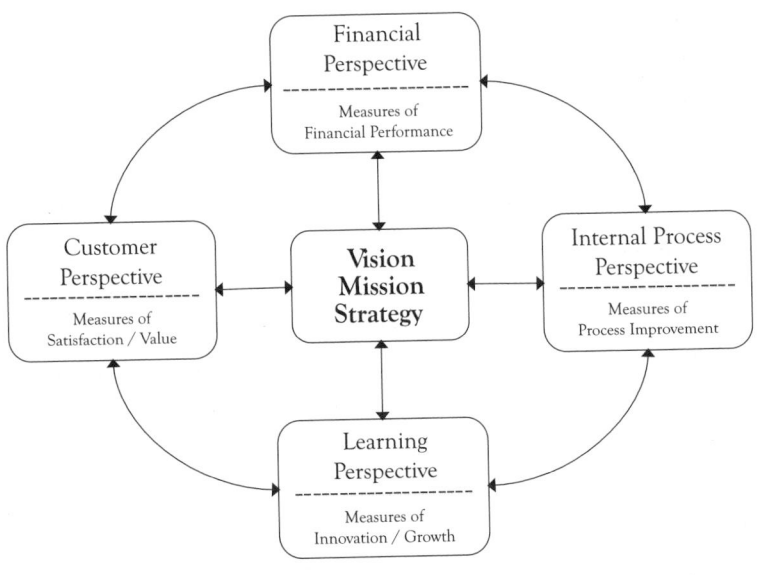

Figure 5.1. The balanced scorecard model.

Adapted with permission of Harvard Business School Press.

From *The Balanced Scorecard* by Kaplan and Norton, Boston, MA 1996, p. 9.

that are the drivers of future financial performance. This "balanced" view of the business prevents overreliance on financial data in managing a business. After briefly summarizing Kaplan and Norton's model, we will look at Serv-Pro's balanced scorecard approach to illustrate application of the concept from a small business perspective.

The balanced scorecard diagram in Figure 5.1 presents four sets of measures that relate to one another and align with a company's vision, mission, and strategy. The *financial perspective* summarizes how the company's strategy implementation is contributing to financial performance. Typical financial measures have to do with profitability, growth, and shareholder value. The *customer perspective* includes measures of how a firm creates value for its customers, such as on-time delivery or the perceived quality of a product or service. Measures related to customer satisfaction such as customer retention or new customer acquisition may also be included in the customer category. The *internal process perspective* evaluates the processes the company uses to deliver its product or service to its customer. This category measures continuous improvement on key activities and core competencies related to strategy, such as new product development or manufacturing productivity. The final category, the *learning perspective*, measures how a firm is building its knowledge base and the ability to grow and change. These measures evaluate a company's continuous development of its knowledge capital—the people, systems, and culture that will enable the company to grow and respond to new challenges in the future. Of course, the actual measures used by each firm will be different, depending on the type of business and its unique strategy. Table 5.2 provides some example balanced scorecard measures for a manufacturing firm.

While the scorecard diagram illustrates the principle of balance in business measures, for strategic purposes it is useful to think of the four perspectives as a cause-and-effect chain, connecting desired outcomes with the drivers of those results. According to Kaplan and Norton,

> Balanced scorecards tell you the knowledge, skills, and systems that your employees will need (their learning and growth) to innovate and build the right strategic capabilities and efficiencies (the internal processes) that deliver specific value to the market (the customers), which will eventually lead to higher shareholder value (the financials).[5]

Table 5.2. Example Scorecard Measures (Manufacturing)

Perspective	Objective	Example strategic measure
Financial	Profitability	Return on capital invested (%)
Customer	Preferred supplier	Customer retention rate (%)
Internal processes	Service	In-stock condition (%)
Learning	Productivity	Contribution margin per employee

Serv-Pro finds the cause-and-effect concept useful and has created a flow chart to show how their selected balanced scorecard measures link to the key action goals for each balanced scorecard perspective—all supporting the strategy of focused differentiation and targeting the vision of the business (see Figure 5.2).

To understand the diagram, start at the bottom with the learning and growth perspective, the foundation of any long-term strategy. As a labor-intensive service business, Serv-Pro determined that consistent investment in two areas—their people and innovation in information technology applications—is essential to success. The company measures their commitment to training and development with a simple metric: direct training expenditures as a percentage of payroll. The commitment to the research and development (R&D) of new technology has a separate line on the annual budget and tracks as a percentage to sales. The actual target for each of these measures is determined based on experience and industry benchmarks. For example, the target for the ongoing training investment is currently 2.5% of payroll dollars (excluding benefits and taxes). Trade association research related to workplace learning indicates that the most profitable service companies invest, on average, around 2.1% of payroll in training and development.[6] Because Serv-Pro seeks to differentiate through execution and service excellence and believes that their people represent a competitive edge, the senior team determined to invest at a rate higher than the norm.[7] The strategic initiative to upgrade the selection, training, and support of the key account manager position fits in this perspective.

You can think through the cause-and-effect logic of the investment in learning and technology using the diagram in Figure 5.2. For example, increasing employee knowledge, skills, and attitudes contributes to better execution of internal processes, which in turn leads to better execution

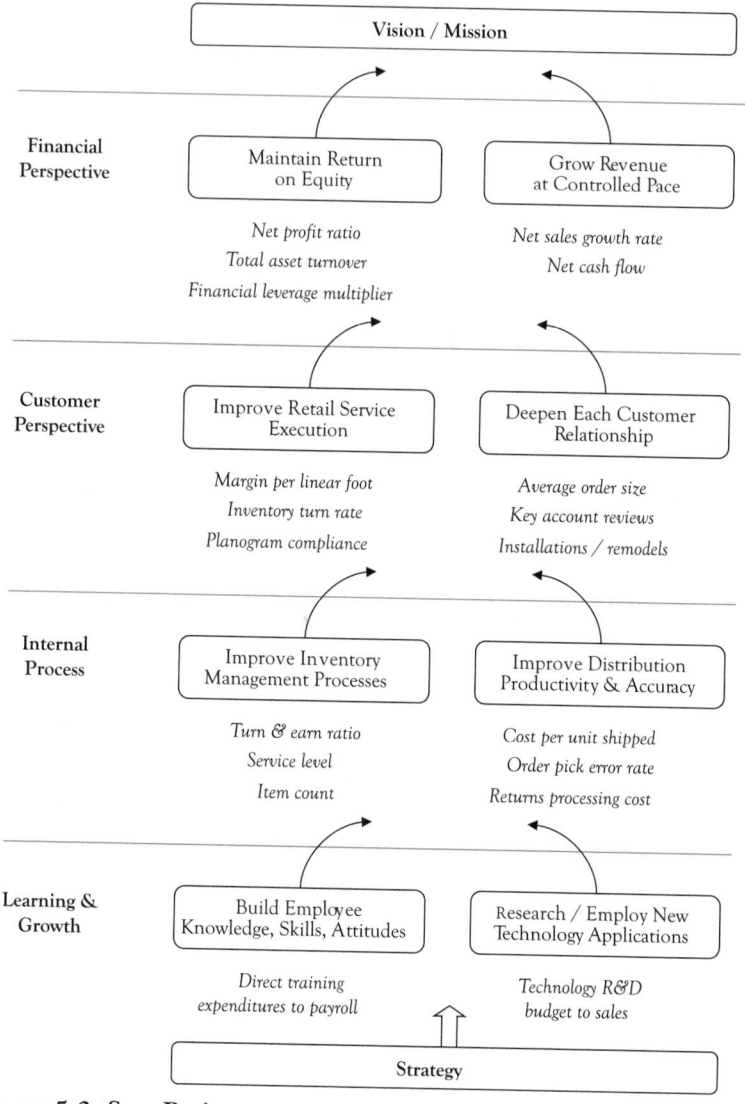

Figure 5.2. Serv-Pro's success measures and their link to strategy.

at retail level and greater customer satisfaction, which ultimately translates to better financials. In the same manner, management information systems and new technology tools, such as bar code scanning devices, improve internal productivity, support execution at retail, facilitate real-time communication and reporting to both management and customers, and help monitor customer profitability. Two of the company's strategic initiatives—the new truck-routing system and further automation of the activity-based costing process—relate to technology innovation.

At the internal process level, the company must support its strategic commitment to a broad and deep inventory selection in specialty foods by paying particular attention to inventory management. The company selected three indicators for monitoring process improvements in inventory management: turn and earn index (inventory turn rate multiplied by gross margin at the item and category levels), service level (% in stock condition), and item count (fixed by product category according to the largest space allocation at retail—item additions require item deletions). In regard to distribution (order production and delivery), operational effectiveness is the goal, finding ways to pick and deliver 10,000 stock-keeping units better, faster, and at a lower cost. The metrics here relate to productivity (cost per unit) and accuracy (error rate). In concert with the new initiative to reduce the amount and cost of processing returns, management added a new measure to determine and track the true cost of processing returns.

From the customer perspective, Serv-Pro focuses on measurements related to the centerpiece of its differentiation strategy: providing excellence in service execution and deepening the long-term relationship with each customer through customized logistic solutions and key account management. To demonstrate the type of execution valued by their supermarket customers, the company developed an innovative process for tracking and reporting by store and by product category such key retail metrics as margin dollars per linear foot, inventory turn rate, and planogram compliance. Serv-Pro's sales merchandiser compensation is based, in part, on improving those numbers. On the relationship side, increasing the average order size per store serves as a customer satisfaction indicator (and provides a big boost to distribution productivity). The company also monitors completion of regular quarterly business reviews and the on-time, on-budget completion of store installations and remodels as important contributors to positive customer relationships.

Finally, the financial perspective focuses on metrics meaningful, in this case, to a privately held business. The ultimate measure is return on equity (investment), which is a function of net profit (revenue/cost stream), asset turnover, and financial leverage (total assets to total equity).

On the revenue side, the company's strategy calls for a controlled growth rate and careful attention to maintaining a positive net cash flow.

The metrics and rationale for your company will be different, but the principles inherent in the balanced scorecard and the process of linking your measures to your organization's strategy are universal. Selecting a limited number of critical indicators within each of the four perspectives keeps everyone focused on the strategy and vision. This focus does not mean your people do not need or use other financial and operational measures at the functional level in the management of your business, just that you have selected the scorecard measures as the "strategic" indicators.

Communicating Your Strategy

In conclusion, think about using your strategic action plans and your balanced scorecard as communication tools to educate all your employees (and other stakeholders as appropriate) about your strategic plan. After all, they are the ones who have to execute it. Communicating will be easier if you have had broad participation in the development of your strategy and the creation of the action plans and success measures.

Put together a systematic communication program that goes beyond the typical onetime events such as the printing and distribution of a brochure or a "town hall" meeting. The best approach is interactive small group meetings led by a member of senior management and one or two team members who participated in the development of the plan. Review and interpret the vision and mission statements. Talk through what you learned in your external and internal analysis. Explain the company's strategic positioning using the "four box" model. Show how the action plans and balanced scorecard embody the strategy. Most important, help the employees link their own activities and metrics to the scorecard measures. For example, a warehouse order picker needs to understand how his or her productivity and accuracy affect the internal process measures and influence customer satisfaction, as well as the financial well-being of the organization. A sales merchandiser needs to see the cost impact of sloppy ordering that results in unnecessary product returns. Some companies even help employees develop personal scorecards to help translate the objectives into meaningful tasks and targets for themselves.[8]

Consider using bulletin boards and electronic media to keep everyone posted as you regularly update scorecard results. Reference the strategy, action plans, and scorecard measures regularly in meetings and discussions. Over time, as you become satisfied that you have the right measures on your scorecard (as evidenced by improving financials) and that you are generating valid and reliable data for the selected measures, consider linking your recognition and reward systems to scorecard results.

Above all, listen to your employees and customers. Action plans and scorecards provide a framework for managing the implementation of strategy, but they also set up a feedback and learning mechanism. Use periodic review sessions to evaluate the causal relationships assumed by the strategy and the quality of execution. If employees are delivering on the performance drivers but the financial numbers are not moving or customers are unhappy, then something is wrong, either with the selected metrics or with the strategy itself, perhaps due to fast-moving changes in the competitive environment. Like the dashboard controls in your car, a strategic plan supported by appropriate controls and measures gives you real-time feedback on performance and an early warning system for potential problems.

With strategic planning, you can control your destiny and guide your business toward profitable achievement of your vision. Follow the process and remember the strategic mantra for small business: *be focused, be different, and be better.*

Notes

Introduction

1. See http://www.sba.gov/size for a summary of the various size standards and how they vary by industry.

2. See, for example, Aragón-Sánchez and Sánchez-Marín (2005); Kraus, Harms, and Schwarz (2006); Robinson and Pearce (1984); and Woods and Joyce (2003).

Chapter 1

1. http://www.famous-quotes-and-quotations.com/yogi-berra-quotes.html

2. Lipton (1996).

3. See Google.com, Microsoft.com, and Amazon.com. It is interesting that in 2008 Microsoft, reflecting the dynamics of the marketplace, changed their vision to a broader statement: "Create experiences that combine the magic of software with the power of Internet services across a world of devices."

4. Fowler and Trachtenberg (2009).

5. Waters (2005), p. 3. See also an interview with Alice Waters titled "Relentless Idealism for Tough Times" in *Harvard Business Review*, June 2009.

6. Collins and Porras (1996), p. 70. The "five whys" technique was originally developed by Toyota Motors and taught to their employees as a tool to address root causes of problems in the production system.

7. Serv-Pro will serve as a case study throughout the book to provide continuity in illustrating various strategic-planning concepts and principles. The company represents a composite of several companies I have worked with during my career in the service distribution industry.

8. Adapted from Collins and Porras (1996) and Lipton (2003).

9. Drucker (2001).

10. Lipton (2003).

11. See http://www.bbbs.org. The most recent strategic plan for Big Brothers Big Sisters reflects revised vision and mission statements, which, in my opinion, are not as effective as the original because they tend to blur the difference between vision and mission. The revised statement for vision reads, "Successful mentoring relationships for all children who need and want them, contributing

to brighter futures, better schools, and stronger communities for all." The mission statement reads, "To help children reach their potential through professionally supported, one-to-one relationships with mentors that have a measurable impact on youth."

12. This section on the key mission questions draws heavily from Peter Drucker's groundbreaking book *Management: Tasks, Responsibilities, Practices* (1974), pp. 74–94.

13. The questions are adapted from Drucker (1974) and Hill and Jones (2008). Figure 1.1 is my original design, integrating the questions from the two sources.

14. Drucker (1974), p. 85.

15. See http://www.aboutyouinc.com/about.htm. Jennifer Kahnweiler is also the author of *The Introverted Leader: Building on Your Quiet Strength* (Berrett-Koehler, 2009).

16. Marklewicz, D. (2009, June 16). See also http://www.nfinity.com.

17. Cathy (2007). See also http://www.chick-fil-a.com.

18. Collins and Porras (1996).

19. Adapted in part from O'Hallaron and O'Hallaron (1999). See also http://www.chick-fil-a.com. The statements on customer focus and quality are from Truett Cathy's "few simple rules" that are part of his "secrets to success."

20. Collins and Porras (1996).

21. Schein (1991).

Chapter 2

1. This paragraph draws from Bradford and Duncan (2000), who provide an extensive discussion on how to create strategic planning teams.

2. Ash (1984), p. 73.

3. The concepts related to general environment forces were drawn primarily from Hill and Jones (2008) and Ireland, Hoskisson, and Hitt (2006).

4. Friedman (2009), p. A19.

5. See http://www.biggreenenergy.com.

6. Gunther (2007) and Fine (2007).

7. Wingfield (2009).

8. Planograns are diagrams or pictures that show item selection and product arrangement at retail level.

9. Barris (2009).

10. Friedman (2007).

11. Aeppel (2009).

12. Dvorak (2007).

13. The soft drink industry example was adapted from Hill and Jones (2008).

14. The definitions and discussions on the five forces that follow are adapted from Porter (1985) and Porter (2008).

15. Michaels (2009).

16. Bradford and Duncan (2000), p. 48.

Chapter 3

1. For a more complex discussion of internal analysis using a concept called "value chains," see Porter (1985).

2. The examples of operational activities and support activities are adapted from Huff, Floyd, Sherman, and Terjesen (2009); see also Porter (1985).

3. For a good introduction to innovation for the small business, see Drucker (2006).

4. The U.S. Small Business Administration (http://www.sba.gov) provides excellent resources on financial management for the small business. Ernest "Bud" Miller, former Dean of the School of Business at Clayton State University, provided direction for including this brief discussion of financial considerations as part of internal analysis.

5. Spors (2009); see also Case (1995).

Chapter 4

1. Porter (1985).

2. The discussion on strategic positioning principles draws primarily from Porter (1996, 2001).

3. See http://www.tervis.com. The Tervis example is based on an interview with Laura Spencer, CEO of Tervis Tumbler.

4. See http://www.catcareoffayette.com. The Cat Care example draws from discussions with Monika Klingler, an MBA student who wrote a paper on Cat Care, and an interview with Dr. Lori Stearns, Cat Care's founder.

5. Colvin (2009).

6. See Porter (1996) and Collis and Rukstad (2008) for more activity map examples.

7. Suggested by Porter (1996), p. 72.

Chapter 5

1. Hackman (2002).

2. Drucker (1974).

3. Gjerde and Hughes (2007).

4. Kaplan and Norton (1996a).

5. Kaplan and Norton (2000), p. 169.

6. ASTD (American Society for Training & Development), the international association for workplace learning professionals, produces an annual state-of-the-industry report that provides industry-specific data on key indicators such as expenditures on employee development.

7. Baron and Shane (2008) provide an excellent resource for ideas on recruiting, selecting, and motivating high-performing employees.

8. Kaplan and Norton (1996b).

References

Aeppel, T. (2009, April 6). As manufacturers buckle, winners emerge from havoc. *Wall Street Journal*, p. B1.

Aragón-Sánchez, A., & Sánchez-Marín, G. (2005). Strategic orientation, management characteristics, and performance: A study of Spanish SMEs. *Journal of Small Business Management, 43*(3), 287–308.

Ash, M. K. (1984). *Mary Kay on people management*. New York: Warner Books.

Baron, R. S., & Shane, S. (2008). *Growing your business: Making human resources work for you*. New York: Business Expert Press.

Barris, M. (2009, May 27). AutoZone profit rises 9.5% on solid sales. *Wall Street Journal*, p. B2.

Bradford, R. W., & Duncan, J. P. (2000). *Simplified strategic planning*. Worcester, MA: Chandler House Press.

Case, J. (1995). *Open-book management: The coming business revolution*. New York: HarperCollins.

Cathy, S. T. (2007). *How did you do it, Truett?* Decatur, GA: Looking Glass Books.

Collins, J. C., & Porras, J. I. (1996, September–October). Building your company's vision. *Harvard Business Review, 74*, 65–77.

Collis, D. J., & Rukstad, M. G. (2008, April). Can you say what your strategy is? *Harvard Business Review, 86*, 82–90.

Colvin, G. (2009, March 16). The world's most admired companies 2009. *Fortune*, 76–78.

Drucker, P. F. (1974). *Management: Tasks, responsibilities, practices*. New York: Harper & Row.

Drucker, P. F. (2001). *The essential Drucker*. New York: Harper-Collins.

Drucker, P. F. (2006). *Innovation and entrepreneurship*. New York: Harper Paperbacks.

Dvorak, P. (2007, November 5). Small firms hire guides as they head abroad. *Wall Street Journal*, B3.

Fine, J. (2007, July 23). When do you stop the presses? *BusinessWeek*, 20.

Fowler, G. A., & Trachtenberg, J. A. (2009, February 10). New Kindle audio feature causes a stir. *Wall Street Journal*, p. B9.

Friedman, T. (2007). *The world is flat 3.0: A brief history of the twenty-first century*. New York: Picador.

Friedman, T. (2009, July 5). U.S. should invest in energy technologies. *Atlanta Journal-Constitution*, p. A19.

Gjerde, K. P., & Hughes, S. B. (2007). Tracking performance: When less is more. *Management Accounting Quarterly, 9*, 1–12.

Gunther, M. (2007, August 6). Hard news. *Fortune*, 80–85.

Hackman, J. R. (2002). *Leading teams: Setting the stage for great performances.* Boston: Harvard Business School Press.

Hill, C., & Jones, G. (2008). *Essentials of strategic management.* New York: Houghton Mifflin.

Huff. A. S., Floyd, S. W., Sherman, H. D., & Terjesen, S. (2009). *Strategic management: Logic and action.* Hoboken, NJ: John Wiley & Sons.

Ireland, R. D., Hoskisson, R. E., & Hitt, M. A. (2006). *Understanding business strategy.* Mason, OH: Thomson South-Western.

Kaplan, R. S., & Norton, D. P. (1996a). *The balanced scorecard: Translating strategy into action.* Boston: Harvard Business School Press.

Kaplan, R. S., & Norton, D. P. (1996b, January–February). Using the balanced scorecard as a strategic management system. *Harvard Business Review, 74*, 75–85.

Kaplan, R. S., & Norton, D. P. (2000, September–October). Having trouble with your strategy? Then map it. *Harvard Business Review, 78*, 167–176.

Kraus, S., Harms, R., & Schwarz, E. J. (2006). Strategic planning in smaller enterprises—new empirical findings. *Management Research News, 29*(6), 334.

Lipton, M. (1996, Summer). Demystifying the development of an organizational vision. *Sloan Management Review, 37*, 83–92.

Lipton, M. (2003). *Guiding growth: How vision keeps companies on course.* Boston: Harvard Business School Press.

Marklewicz, D. (2009, June 16). Stand-up guy for female feet. *Atlanta Journal-Constitution*, pp. A7–A8.

Michaels, D. (2009, July 2). Airline sector's woes slam a highflier. *Wall Street Journal*, p. A1.

O'Hallaron, R., & O'Hallaron, D. (1999). *The mission primer: Four steps to an effective mission statement.* Richmond, VA: Mission Incorporated.

Porter, M. E. (1985). *Competitive advantage: Creating and sustaining superior performance.* New York: Free Press.

Porter, M. E. (1996, November–December). What is strategy? *Harvard Business Review, 74*, 61–78.

Porter, M. E. (2001, March). Strategy and the Internet. *Harvard Business Review, 79*, 62–78.

Porter, M. E. (2008, January). The five competitive forces that shape strategy. *Harvard Business Review, 86*, 78–93.

Robinson, R. B., Jr., & Pearce, J. A., II. (1984). Research thrusts in small firm strategic planning. *Academy of Management Review, 9*(1), 128–137.

Schein, E. H. (1991). *Organizational culture and leadership.* San Francisco: Jossey-Bass.

Spors, K. K. (2009). Top small workplaces 2009. *Wall Street Journal,* p. R4.

Waters, A. (2005). The delicious revolution. Retrieved June 9, 2009, from http:// www.chezpanisse.com

Wingfield, N. (2009, June 23). Netflix boss plots life after DVD. *Wall Street Journal,* pp. A1, A12.

Woods, A., & Joyce, P. (2003). Owner-managers and the practice of strategic management. *International Small Business Journal, 21*(2), 181–195.

Index